GUARDING THE GOSPEL OF GRACE

Contending for the Faith
in the
Face of Compromise

(Galatians and Jude)

by David M. Levy

The Friends of Israel Gospel Ministry, Inc.
P. O. Box 908, Bellmawr, NJ 08099

GUARDING THE GOSPEL OF GRACE:
CONTENDING FOR THE FAITH IN THE FACE OF
COMPROMISE
(Galatians and Jude)

The Friends of Israel Gospel Ministry, Inc.
P. O. Box 908, Bellmawr, New Jersey 08099

Cover by Left Coast Designs, Portland, OR

DEDICATION

This book is dedicated to all of the faithful men and women throughout church history who were steadfast and unmovable in their proclamation and defense of the gospel of grace—those who guarded the purity of the gospel with their very lives, of whom the world was not worthy.

CONTENTS

PREFACE

The growth of the occult and cult practices has been rampant in recent years. Those engaged in cult-watching estimate that more than 3,000 man-made Eastern philosophical religious systems have sprung up throughout America. They are not only across town, but down the street—and often thriving right next door.

Our nation is being inundated with books and videos on the occult. Walk into any major book store and you will be amazed at the large selection of books dealing with reincarnation, astrology, Scientology, holistic medicine, positive or possibility thinking, psychotherapy, the New Age movement, and self-improvement success motivation techniques—to name just a few. Each book explains how the author's so-called "gospel" is the true way to happiness and fulfillment in life.

Surf the channels on late night television and you will find programs on astrology, horoscopes, spiritism, and psychic readings luring viewers to seek a fuller meaning of life by embracing certain psychic practices. All you need do is dial the number flashing on the television screen, and—for a fee—a counselor from the Psychic Friends Network will provide you with information concerning your future. Testimonials are given by smiling television and movie personalities who have supposedly benefited from psychic readings.

At the time of this writing, a cult called *Heaven's Gate*, originated by Marshall Herff Applewhite, the son of a Presbyterian minister, is making front-page news. Applewhite, along with his cofounder, Bonnie Lu Trusdale Nettles, known by their followers as "Do" and "Ti," began their movement in 1970. Their beliefs were an odd mixture of Christian teachings, early Gnosticism, New Age mysticism, science fiction, Eastern religions, astrology, Mormonism, and

Scientology. Marshall Applewhite believed that he was Jesus Christ, the Son of God, and that Bonnie Nettles was God the Father. Applewhite taught that they had returned to earth as "Father" and "Son" to offer people the opportunity to acquire a unique salvation on a metaphysical level in the kingdom of heaven. Applewhite believed that the discovery of the Hale-Bopp Comet sent a "red alert" to members of Heaven's Gate that a spaceship (UFO) was coming to transport them to their promised destiny. On March 26, 1997, members of the Heaven's Gate cult made the conscious decision to shed their earthly bodies by committing suicide, so that their souls could be transported by the supposed UFO to the "higher kingdom of heaven."

"Just another crazy cult full of nonsensical religious jargon," you say? Not to the 39 highly intelligent devotees of Heaven's Gate who were taken in by the twisted teachings of their leader. Lost souls looking for ways to fill the God-shaped void in their hearts were duped into following this false messiah. These people were looking for meaning, purpose, and release from the emptiness and despair of their sin-filled hearts. This is not a unique incident but a harbinger of things to come as we near the new millennium. Among many of the cults in America, there is a growing sense that life as we know it on planet Earth will end by the year 2000.

Christians are often unaware of the teachings and tactics of cults. Their teachings are often subtly altered, peppered with enough Christian truth to gain acceptance within Christianity. All too often, Christians are unconsciously conditioned to believe and practice the anti-biblical teachings that surround them. Lest you think that this does not happen, think again! While writing this preface, I received a telephone call from a pastor friend who related an incident that occurred in his church. During a men's prayer breakfast he noticed two visitors talking to some of the church members in a corner of the room. Upon closer examination he found that

they were from a group called "Israelites"—modern-day
Judaizers who believe that we must keep the law and ceremonial practices found in Judaism to be Christians. They
crept into the prayer breakfast, came alongside these men,
and were using the opportunity to spread their heretical
teaching.

Today Christian leaders have unlimited access to propagate their gospel worldwide through print, radio, television,
and the Internet. Many see themselves as luminaries of the
truth to whom God has given special gifts to direct, teach,
and heal their followers. Christians often flock to such people, believing that God has indeed given them special revelation that will bring extraordinary blessings through health,
wealth, advancement in employment, or greater knowledge
of God by some existential religious experience. These self-
styled prophets often build their ministries on ideas developed through their own visions, dreams, prophecies, and
novel opinions, which are in direct contradiction to Scripture.
Over time, such teachers prove to be nothing more than fall-
en stars who streak across the religious world for a season
and then vanish into disgraceful obscurity. Sad to say, their
followers are often gullible, unassuming, and spiritually
immature, having itching ears to learn but unable to discern
truth from error. Such people are vulnerable and open to the
control of heretical leaders.

To hold up a standard against the flood of anti-Christian
teaching sweeping the nation, Christians need a proper
understanding of the Bible and its doctrinal teaching.
Unfortunately, many Christians believe that too much
emphasis is placed on doctrine. "Doctrine," they say,
"divides people, but love unites." True, love must be emphasized within the church, but not at the expense of correct doctrine. Such Christians are often weak and fuzzy in their
thinking about what their faith teaches. When asked to
explain the doctrine of God, Christ, the Holy Spirit, sin, grace,

regeneration, justification, sanctification, or last things, they are hard-pressed to give an answer. Many are tossed to and fro with every wind of doctrine and have fallen prey to the myriad of false beliefs being proclaimed in some churches and in the media. Sadder still, some so-called Christians seem to lack the spiritual discernment needed to fend off present-day heresies. There are few dissenting voices alerting people to guard against the other gospels being proclaimed.

These problems are not new to the church. They are the offspring of similar heresies faced by the apostles soon after the church was established. The Apostle Paul was quick to warn the fledgling church about false teachers who came as angels of light peddling heresy: "For I know this, that after my departing shall grievous wolves enter in among you, not sparing the flock. Also of your own selves shall men arise, speaking perverse things, to draw away disciples after them...for the space of three years I ceased not to warn everyone night and day with tears" (Acts 20:29-31). It was for reasons like this that Paul wrote the Epistle to the Galatians and Jude wrote the epistle bearing his name. These two men were led by the Holy Spirit to *guard the gospel of grace* by addressing major heretical issues that would be faced by the church.

Although small in size, few books have impacted the world as have Galatians and Jude. Merrill C. Tenney writes, "Christianity might have been just one more Jewish sect, and the thought of the Western world might have been entirely pagan had it [Galatians] never been written. Galatians embodies the germinal teaching on Christian freedom which separated Christianity from Judaism, and which launched it upon a career of missionary conquest. It was the cornerstone of the Protestant Reformation, because its teaching of salvation by grace alone became the dominant theme of the preaching of the Reformers...It has been called 'the Magna Charta of spiritual emancipation,' for on its principles is formed the whole faith of a free church"

(Tenney, *Galatians: The Charter of Christian Liberty*, 1954, pp. 15-16).

The message of Galatians and Jude is of primary importance in the church today for several reasons. First, both books deal with the question of *legalism*. In the past 25 years, thousands of Jewish people have come to faith in Jesus as their Messiah. Understanding that they were saved, not by law, but by grace, many Jewish believers struggle with how much credence to give to the law. It should be noted that Jewish people who have put their faith in Christ do not cease to be Jews. However, Paul made it very clear that Jewish believers find their identity in keeping the teachings of Christ, not the religious laws, teachings, and ceremonies of Judaism. Paul was careful to show that all believers—Jewish and Gentile alike—are under no obligation to keep any portion of the Mosaic or Oral Law. Christ's death on the cross abrogated any relationship that people have to the Mosaic Law as a rule of life over them. Although believers are not under the law, they will fulfill the righteousness of God contained in the law through living out the biblical teachings of Christ by grace through faith.

It should be noted that the church is independent from Israel and should not be identified as a sect within Judaism. Nor does Scripture teach that the church is a replacement for natural Israel, often called "spiritual Israel." The church is a distinct entity standing independent from God's program for Israel.

Second, both books deal with the question of *Christian liberty*. Paul said, "Stand fast...in the liberty with which Christ hath made us free, and be not entangled again with the yoke of bondage" (5:1). Believers are justified by grace through faith and have a perfect standing before God. They have been set free from the law and are to be led by the Holy Spirit in their walk of faith. Therefore, submission to the law would not benefit Christians. In fact, it would only lead to bondage. The whole purpose of Christ's death on the cross is to forever free people from the enslavement of the law, which could never bring them into a perfect standing before God.

Third, both books deal with the question of *licentious living*. Paul said, "brethren, ye have been called unto liberty; only use not liberty for an occasion to the flesh" (5:13). Freedom in Christ does not mean that there are no limits or bounds for believers, nor is it an excuse for people to live as they so desire. Even God, who is the source of every Christian's freedom, is limited by His holiness. Judaizers would argue that Christians need the restraining influence of the law to hold their sin nature in check. Paul states just the opposite. The key to overcoming the sin nature is not through law-keeping or self-effort, but through the indwelling power of the Holy Spirit, who enables believers to live holy lives. Christians who yield to the Holy Spirit's control moment by moment will not succumb to licentious living (5:16-19, 22-25; 6:8).

Fourth, both books send a warning to *leaders* who pervert the teaching of liberty. Paul focused his attention on denouncing the Judaizers' teaching that Gentile Christians must keep the ceremonial practices of Judaism, especially circumcision. Jude focused on false teachers who were just the opposite: morally degenerate people who crept into the church and perverted the gospel of grace. These people taught that Christians had license to live as they pleased because their sins would not be held against them.

The gospel, when properly explained, will defend itself. But to properly guard the gospel against the onslaught of heretical religious systems, Christians must know how to rightly divide the word of truth. The books of Galatians and Jude should not only be read, they should be studied. It is my prayer that this volume will properly equip you to guard and defend the gospel of grace.

PART I

GALATIANS

INTRODUCTION

The church has recognized Paul as the author of Galatians; internal and external evidence validates this fact. In chapters 1 and 2, Paul presents an autobiographical profile of his life and ministry, proving his call to be an apostle. Galatians definitely bears marks of Paul's authorship in style, phraseology, and teaching. Early church fathers such as Clement of Rome, Polycarp, Barnabas, Hermas, and Ignatius quote Paul as the author of Galatians.

At its inception, the church was composed mostly of Jewish people, but soon the gospel spread and Gentile converts were added to the fellowship. This raised questions concerning the Gentiles' relationship to Jewish believers, the Law of Moses, circumcision, and a host of other cultural practices. Judaizers began to infiltrate the churches of Galatia, teaching that for Gentiles to be truly saved they must keep certain Mosaic laws. Some of the Galatian believers heeded the Judaizers' message and were on the verge of deserting their position of salvation by faith through grace alone. At the same time, the Judaizers discredited Paul in three ways. They denied his apostleship; they denied the truth of his gospel; and they taught that his message led to corrupt living.

Paul wrote to the Galatians for three reasons: to show that salvation is by grace through faith devoid of keeping the law, which in turn leads to godly living; to defend his apostleship and prove that his authority was from God; and to address and correct the false accusations being made by the Judaizers.

Most scholars agree that Paul wrote his epistle to the churches of Galatia, but they are divided on whether he wrote to the churches in north or south Galatia. Those holding the *Northern Galatian* theory believe that Paul wrote to Gauls who had settled in the north-central part of Asia Minor (Pessinus, Ancyra, and Tavium) in 300 B.C. According to this view, Paul founded churches in the north on his second missionary journey (Acts 16:4-8) and revisited them on his third journey (Acts 18:22-23). This would mean that he wrote his epistle from either Ephesus or Macedonia between 53 and 57 A.D.

Those holding the *Southern Galatian* theory believe that Paul wrote his epistle on his first missionary journey from Antioch of Syria in 48 or 49 A.D. Many scholars hold the Southern Galatian theory, which seems to be more plausible for several reasons. There is no evidence that Paul established churches in northern Galatia, but he did establish churches in Antioch, Iconium, Lystra, and Derbe, which were located in the south. Paul does not mention any decisions made during the Jerusalem council (Acts 15), which was held in either 48 or 49 A.D.; thus, Galatians must have been written just before it was held. Judaizers, rather than traveling to the far north, would have tried to influence the large Jewish population in the south, to whom they had easy access, and Gentile believers as well.

The theme of Galatians is *Christian liberty through the gospel of grace.* Mankind's justification comes from God by grace through faith apart from the works of the law (3:11). Although "the law is holy...just, and good" (Rom. 7:12) and was used to identify sin for mankind, people could not be saved by keeping it. The law showed people that they were guilty and condemned before God and could be saved only by God's grace through faith in Jesus Christ.

Paul illustrated his position of salvation by grace apart from the law in two ways. First, he related his own conversion: "For if I build again the things which I destroyed, I make myself a transgressor. For I, through the law, am dead to the law, that I might live unto God. I am crucified with Christ: nevertheless I live; yet not I, but Christ liveth in me; and the life which I now live in the flesh I live by the faith of the Son of God, who loved me and gave himself for me" (2:18-20). Second, he reviewed the covenant that God made with Abraham: "And this I say, that the covenant that was confirmed before by God in Christ, the law, which was four hundred and thirty years after, cannot annul, that it should make the promise of no effect. For if the inheritance be of the law, it is no more of promise; but God gave it to Abraham by promise" (3:17-18). People are to stand fast in Christian liberty and not allow Judaizers to take them back into the bondage of the Mosaic and Oral Law. "Stand fast, therefore, in the liberty with which Christ hath made us free, and be not entangled again with the yoke of bondage" (5:1).

Some of the key words in Galatians are *law, faith, gospel, flesh,* and *Spirit.* The two key verses in the book are 3:10-11: "For as many as are of the works of the law are under the curse; for it is written, Cursed is everyone that continueth not in all things which are written in the book of the law, to do them. But that no man is justified by the law in the sight of God, it is evident; for, The just shall live by faith" (cp. 5:1).

OUTLINE

I. PAUL'S DECLARATION (1:1-5)
  A. Apostleship (1:1)
  B. Associates (1:2)
  C. Address (1:3)
  D. Atonement (1:3-4)
    1. Savior (1:3)
    2. Sacrifice (1:4)
    3. Salvation (1:4)
    4. Sovereign (1:4)
  E. Adoration (1:5)
  F. Affirmation (1:5)

II. PAUL'S DEFENSE (1:6-2:21)
  A. Denouncing Apostasy (1:6-9)
    1. Departure from the Truth (1:6)
    2. Different Teaching (1:6)
    3. Disturbing Teachers (1:7)
    4. Distorting Truth (1:7)
    5. Destroying Truth (1:8)
    6. Damned Teachers (1:8-9)
  B. Defense of the Apostle (1:10-24)
    1. Paul's Motive (1:10)
    2. Paul's Message (1:11-12)
    3. Paul's Manner of Life (1:13-14)
    4. Paul's Ministry (1:15-17)
    5. Paul's Mission (1:18-24)
  C. Demonstration of Apostolic Authority (2:1-10)
    1. Church Council (2:1-3)
    2. Church Charlatans (2:4)
    3. Church Commitment (2:5)
    4. Church Conference (2:6)

Paul, an apostle (not of men, neither by man, but by Jesus Christ, and God the Father, who raised him from the dead), And all the brethren who are with me, unto the churches of Galatia: Grace be to you, and peace, from God the Father, and from our Lord Jesus Christ, Who gave himself for our sins, that he might deliver us from this present evil age, according to the will of God and our Father, To whom be glory for ever and ever. Amen. I marvel that ye are so soon removed from him that called you into the grace of Christ unto another gospel, Which is not another; but there are some that trouble you, and would pervert the gospel of Christ. But though we, or an angel from heaven, preach any other gospel unto you than that which we have preached unto you, let him be accursed. As we said before, so say I now again, If any man preach any other gospel unto you than that ye have received, let him be accursed (Galatians 1:1-9).

ONE TRUE GOSPEL

**"...If any man preach any other gospel unto you
than that ye have received,
let him be accursed" (1:9).**

In the past 30 years there has been a proliferation of "new gospels" in the United States. Some are rooted in Eastern philosophical religions, such as Hinduism. Others are based on pop-psychologies, which promise health and happiness to loyal followers through their self-awareness techniques. Still others are perverted forms of Christianity propagated by charismatic leaders who possess total control over their faithful followers through their heretical teachings. All of these religious systems claim to possess the one true gospel (good news) for mankind.

Paul faced a similar problem in his day. Judaizers had crept into the churches of Galatia, denying Paul's apostolic authority and preaching "another gospel" (v. 6)—mixing law with grace.

The apostle wasted no time. Taking pen in hand, he opened his letter to the Galatians with the customary salutation, but he omitted any mention of praise or prayer on behalf of the Galatian believers to whom he was writing. Instead, he launched into a declaration of his apostolic authority, a sharp rebuke of the Galatians for their departure from the faith, and a denouncement of the heretical teachers.

Apostleship Declared

Immediately Paul set the record straight concerning his authority: "Paul, an apostle (not of [Gr., *from*] men, neither by [Gr., *through*] man, but [strong contrast] by [Gr., *through*] Jesus Christ, and God the Father, who raised him from the dead)" (v. 1).

The word *apostle* means *to send forth* or *one commissioned by another to represent him in some way*. An apostle was a representative of Christ who had been chosen, called, given credentials, and commissioned to take His message to whomever he was sent. Three things were necessary to qualify for apostleship: The individual had to be personally chosen and called to his position by the Lord; he had to have seen the resurrected Lord; and he received his commission, authority, and message from Christ.

Paul met all of these qualifications, as verse 1 reveals. First, he did not receive his apostleship and authority "from" any man. Second, neither did he appoint himself to be an apostle. Third, no human agent sent him out. The Godhead was the only source, the direct agent who called and commissioned him to be an apostle. The preposition "by" and the conjunction "and" indicate that Jesus is coequal and coeternal with "God the Father," as well as the sending agent. Fourth, Paul never met an apostle until after God had commissioned him to his position (vv. 17-18). Fifth, Paul's statement in verse 1 sets him apart from the false prophets and ranks him with the 12 who were commissioned directly by the Lord.

Paul sent a greeting to the Galatians from "all the brethren" (v. 2) with whom he was traveling. Although he did not identify his traveling companions, many commentators believe they were Barnabas and others from the church at Antioch (Acts 13:1).

He addressed all "the churches of Galatia" (v. 2). Paul expected this letter to be circulated and read in cities such as Antioch, Lystra, Derbe, and Iconium, where he had established churches during his first missionary journey.

The apostle's salutation incorporated the standard greeting of the day, "Grace be to you, and peace" (v. 3). The word *grace* was the usual greeting for the Greeks, as was *peace* for the Jewish people. These two words encompassed what both groups had experienced in salvation. Salvation came through *grace* and produced *peace* in their hearts. The source of both was "from God the Father, and from our Lord Jesus Christ" (v. 3). God's grace and peace sustain believers in their daily walk with the Lord. Later in his letter Paul informed the Galatians that if they succumbed to the legalism being propagated by false teachers, they would fall from grace and forfeit the peace they had once experienced from God.

Atonement Described

The apostle concluded his salutation by reminding the Galatians of God's redemptive program on their behalf. First, salvation did not come by the works of the law, but through the Savior, the "Lord Jesus Christ" (v. 3).

Second, Christ's atoning death was sacrificial. No one coerced Him to die for sin; He freely "gave himself" (v. 4) for mankind's sin. Jesus said concerning His life, "No man taketh it from me, but I lay it down of myself. I have power to lay it down, and I have power to take it again. This commandment have I received of my Father" (Jn. 10:18; cp. Jn. 10:15, 17; Heb. 9:14).

Third, His sacrifice was a substitution; Jesus gave

Himself "for our sins" (v. 4). The preposition *for* means that Christ died *instead of* or *on behalf of* mankind. He voluntarily became the sinners' substitute, dying in our place. "For the love of Christ constraineth us, because we thus judge that, if one died for all, then were all dead; And that he died for all, that they who live should not henceforth live unto themselves, but unto him who died for them, and rose again" (2 Cor. 5:14-15). Christ's death in place of sinners perfectly satisfied the just demands of God's holy law, thereby making it possible for God to forgive mankind's sin.[1]

Fourth, His death paid the price for sin (v. 4). People are viewed by God as slaves, sold into the bondage of sin (Rom. 7:14) and under the sentence of death (Jn. 3:18-19; Rom. 6:23). Through Christ's shed blood and death on the cross, the purchase price was paid to buy mankind out of the slave market of sin (Gal. 3:13; 4:5), thus setting them free (Ti. 2:14; 1 Pet. 1:18-19).

Fifth, the purpose of Christ's death was to salvage mankind or "deliver" (*emancipate, rescue*) [v. 4] them from the state of bondage. The word *deliver* was used "by Stephen in...describing the divine deliverance of Joseph and the children of Israel from Egyptian affliction (Acts 7:10, 34). Peter...from prison (Acts 12:11)....Paul from a belligerent mob in Jerusalem" (Acts 23:7).[2]

Sixth, the deliverance is from the power of a satanic system described as "this present evil age" (v. 4). The word *age* refers to the immoral course of this world system, which is being controlled by Satan. It was this "evil" system in which the Galatians had once walked. "And you hath he made alive, who were dead in trespasses and sins; In which in times past ye walked according to the course of this world, according to the prince of the power of the air, the spirit that now worketh in the sons of disobedience; Among whom also we all had our manner of life in times past in the lusts of our flesh, fulfilling the desires of the flesh and of the mind, and were by nature the children of wrath, even as others" (Eph.

2:1-3). Christ had rescued them from this bondage through His once-for-all atoning death on the cross. "But God, who is rich in mercy, for his great love with which he loved us, Even when we were dead in sins, hath made us alive together with Christ (by grace ye are saved)" (Eph. 2:4-5).

Seventh, the Lord is the source of this deliverance provided "according to the will of God" (v. 4). Therefore, Christ delivered mankind from sin, not by any plan put forth through the law, but through the procedure prescribed by the sovereign decree of Almighty God.

Paul concluded his salutation with the affirmation, "To whom be glory for ever and ever. Amen" (v. 5). The apostle's doxology is very appropriate. What believer would not have a heart like his—full of praise for the great salvation provided by the sovereign Godhead? Such salvation will glorify God, not only in this age, but "for ever and ever"— or for the ages of ages. What a contrast to the legalists, whose perverted gospel of legalism will last only for this present evil age!

Paul set the course of his letter to the Galatians in two ways. He declared and defended his apostleship, and he argued that salvation was provided solely through Christ's finished work on the cross, apart from any human work or merit. To add legalism in any form was to pervert the *one true gospel*.

Astounding Desertion

Upon hearing the news that the believers in Galatia were succumbing to the message of the Judaizers, Paul said, "I marvel that ye are so soon removed from him that called you into the grace of Christ" (v. 6). The word *marvel* means to be *amazed, astonished, miffed, bewildered*. It portrays the apostle as speechless and agitated when he heard of the Galatians' defection. He was amazed that they were "so soon" departing from the true gospel. The term *soon* means *quickly* and speaks of how readily, without much thought, the Galatians were leaving their prior commitment to Christ.

They had "removed" (v. 6) themselves from the liberty that the Lord had bestowed on them. The word *removed* means more than just *departing*; it means *to desert*. The term was used in a military sense, such as when people go AWOL or commit mutiny. Paul used the word in the present tense and middle voice, indicating that they were in the process of deserting the Lord on their own. They were deserting not only the doctrinal teaching of salvation by grace through faith, which Paul put forth, but "him" (v. 6)— God Himself.

The Galatians had been "called...into the grace of Christ" (v. 6), an effectual call that had resulted in their salvation. Their salvation came through the "grace of Christ" (v. 6) and was totally unmerited and devoid of any good works that they had accomplished. God had showered down His love, favor, and blessing; to go back to the bondage of the law would have been to desert not only the favor of God but God Himself. Such a departure was unthinkable and bewildering to Paul.

Apostasy Denounced

The different teaching embraced by the Galatians was "another [different kind of] gospel" (v. 6). The word *another* is from the Greek word *heterodoxy*, meaning *another opinion*, from which comes the idea of heresy or false doctrine. Thus, the Galatians were turning to a gospel of heresy or false doctrine. The word *gospel* means *good news* and, in context, refers to the good news of salvation provided through Christ's work on the cross, which was purely by grace, apart from the works of the law. Thus, the legalists' gospel was, of necessity, evil and could not be claimed to be good news or the true gospel. Therefore, it is "not another" gospel at all (v. 7).

Paul then focused his attention on the Judaizers, who were bringing in their heretical teachings and passing them off as the true gospel. The term *Judaizer* comes from the Greek word *ludaizo*, which means *to be* or *to live like a Jew*. The word is not used as a national description of Jewish people, but as a religious designation of those who believed that Gentiles who became Christians should live in accordance with the Mosaic law, ceremonial law, Jewish customs, and tradition. They taught that it was not enough to simply believe in Jesus—which to them was cheap grace—without embracing the practices of Judaism. People who really wanted to be Christians had to be like Jesus: become Jews first and then Christians. Judaizers taught that it was necessary for Gentiles who had received Christ to live like Jews by keeping the ceremonial practices found in Judaism, especially circumcision (Acts 15:1; Gal. 5:2; 6:12-13).

Judaizers tried to discredit Paul's authority as a true apostle. They dogged his footsteps during his missionary ministry, trying to undo his work. They substituted a salvation of works for the salvation that Paul taught, which was by grace through faith in Jesus Christ alone. Paul clearly taught that the Judaizers' beliefs were heretical and that the gospel was not an addendum to Judaism, a mere supplement to the law, but the end and fulfillment of the law and the antithesis to it.

The apostle strongly denounced the Judaizers' motives (4:17; 6:12-13). He called such teachers "dogs...evil workers...the concision" (Phil. 3:2). The word *concision* described pagans who cut their bodies while practicing idolatrous worship. Paul used the term as a play on the Greek word *circumcision*. The "concision" (Judaizers) who wanted the Galatians to be circumcised were actually mutilating the gospel message by mixing the works of the law with grace.

Scholars are divided on whether the Judaizers were saved. Some, like Dr. Kenneth Wuest, call them unsaved

Jews who set up a perverted legalism built around the Mosaic Law.[3] Dr. Richard Longenecker believes that Paul's language in Galatians 1-2 indicates that the Judaizers were saved. He wrote, "From Paul's manner of speaking of the situation in Gal. 1-2, it is difficult to picture these Judaizers as anything but Jewish Christians—in fact, Jewish Christians claiming to represent the official position of the Jerusalem Church....In all probability they were members of the strict law-abiding group in the Jerusalem church."[4] Most commentators are mute on the subject, not stating whether they believe the Judaizers to be saved or unsaved. It seems from Paul's statement in verse 9 that those who were preaching another gospel were to be considered anathema or damned to destruction. Therefore, it is difficult to assume that they were true believers in Christ.

The Judaizers' teachings were wrong for three reasons. First, their teaching disturbed or troubled (v. 7) the Galatians. The word *troubled* means *to be mentally disturbed by fear and confusion*. In other words, the Judaizers were confusing the Galatian churches and undermining their confidence in Christ.

Second, their teachings distorted the truth by "pervert[ing] the gospel of Christ" (v. 7). The word *pervert* means *to reverse, change, turn about*. These heretical teachers were reversing the message of the gospel by changing it from a gospel of grace to a gospel of works—a message diametrically opposed to what God had originally established (Rom. 11:6).

Third, for these teachers to preach any other gospel was to *destroy* the truth: "But though we, or an angel from heaven, preach any other gospel unto you than that which we have preached unto you, let him be accursed" (v. 8). Paul was not teaching that he himself (a divinely called apostle) or a heavenly being was likely ever to preach any other gospel. But, if they were to preach another gospel, let them be accursed (lit., anathema, v. 8), eternally damned to destruction.

The apostle reminded the Galatians that he and others ("we," v. 9) had warned them "before" (v. 9) of such teachers and teachings. The words "said before" (v. 9) mean *to say beforehand*; thus, Paul was contrasting *before* with *now* (v. 9), indicating that verse 9 was not just rehearsing what was said in the previous verse. He reminded the Galatians that he and others had warned them in the past to be on guard against the teachings of such people as the Judaizers. Such a warning would make their desertion even more odious.

In stating, "If any man preach any other gospel unto you...let him be accursed" (v. 9), Paul was not putting forth a hypothetical situation. In their case, it was factual. Paul was pressing home the point that because these Judaizers were preaching another gospel, they were to be considered anathema.

Paul emphatically warned that those who tamper with biblical revelation of the gospel are anathema. Strong and sobering words, these, but they are necessary today. The gospel is being assaulted from every side—twisted, made fun of, embellished, and diminished. The apostle's admonition must be heeded. Turn a deaf ear to the myriad so-called "new gospels" inundating our society and embrace only the *one true gospel*. Remember, if the gospel you hear today is new, it cannot be true; if it is true, it is not new!

ENDNOTES

[1] Kenneth S. Wuest, *Wuest's Word Studies*, Galatians (Grand Rapids: Wm. B. Eerdmans Publishing Co., 1944), p. 33.

[2] John MacArthur, *The MacArthur New Testament Commentary*, Galatians (Chicago: Moody Press, 1987), p. 6.

[3] *Op. Cit.*, Wuest, p. 21.

[4] Richard N. Longenecker, *The Origin and Nature of Paul's Christianity*, Paul, Apostle of Liberty (Grand Rapids: Baker Book House, 1964), pp. 213-214.

For do I now seek the favor of men, or of God? Or do I seek to please men? For if I yet pleased men, I should not be the servant of Christ. But I make known to you, brethren, that the gospel which was preached by me is not after man. For I neither received it of man, neither was I taught it, but by the revelation of Jesus Christ. For ye have heard of my manner of life in time past in the Jews' religion, how that beyond measure I persecuted the church of God, and wasted it; And profited in the Jews' religion above many my equals in mine own nation, being more exceedingly zealous of the traditions of my fathers. But when it pleased God, who separated me from my mother's womb, and called me by his grace, To reveal his Son in me, that I might preach him among the Gentiles, immediately I conferred not with flesh and blood; Neither went I up to Jerusalem to them who were apostles before me, but I went into Arabia, and returned again unto Damascus. Then, after three years, I went up to Jerusalem to see Peter, and abode with him fifteen days. But other of the apostles saw I none, except James, the Lord's brother. Now the things which I write unto you, behold, before God, I lie not. Afterwards I came into the regions of Syria and Cilicia, And was unknown by face unto the churches of Judæa which were in Christ; But they had heard only, He who persecuted us in times past now preacheth the faith which once he destroyed. And they glorified God in me (Galatians 1:10-24).

2

CHOSEN OF GOD

"...they had heard only, He who persecuted us
in times past now preacheth the faith
which once he destroyed" (1:23).

Judaizers had infiltrated the churches of Galatia and
were sowing seeds of dissension. They had tried to
discredit Paul's apostleship by claiming he was a man
pleaser—teaching circumcision when with the Jews (1 Cor.
9:20) but setting aside the practice to make it easier for
Gentiles to receive the gospel. They also accused him of not
being an apostle, stating that he lacked the credentials listed in Acts 1:21-22. These were serious charges, which, if not
dealt with, would severely erode Paul's authority in the
churches of Galatia.

Paul defended his divine call and authority as an apostle by relating to the Galatians his personal testimony
before and after his conversion.

Paul's Motive

Asking two rhetorical questions, Paul condemned such accusations: "For do I now seek the favor of men, or of God? Or do I seek to please men?" (v. 10). Obviously Paul sought to please God! Someone trying to placate others by compromising the gospel would not curse those who preached another gospel, as Paul did (cp. vv. 6-9). Nor would a person suffer privations and persecutions for the gospel, as Paul did (2 Cor. 11:23-28; Gal. 6:17), if he were a compromiser.

Paul made it very clear that if he tried to "please men," he "should not be the servant [bond slave] of Christ" (v. 10). Paul ordered his life so that he would be "accepted of him [lit. *well-pleasing to Christ*]" (2 Cor. 5:9). Actually, it was Paul's accusers who were the men pleasers, making a show of the flesh by having others circumcised so that they would not "suffer persecution for the cross of Christ" (6:12).

Paul's Message

The apostle directed his message to the "brethren" (v. 11) who were being led into heresy by the Judaizers. With forceful words, Paul said, "But I make known to you, brethren, that the gospel which was preached by me is not after man" (v. 11). The word "certify" (v. 11) in the KJV means *to make known* in certain, clear, and convincing language, leaving no doubt of what he meant. Paul set the record straight. He was not proclaiming a man-made religious system originated by himself or others. He did not receive it from any man (v. 12). It was not transmitted to him by either direct or indirect communication from any witness or apostle. True, Paul heard the preaching of Stephen before his conversion (Acts 7), but the gospel he preached was not acquired in that way. "Neither was I taught it" (v. 12), he said. Although he had contact with Ananias and Barnabas after his conversion, he did not receive instruction or interpretation concerning the Word of God from them. Paul received his gospel by direct "revelation of Jesus Christ" (v. 12). The word *revelation* means *to unveil* that which had previously been concealed by God. Hence, the apostle claimed that his revelation came through direct divine disclosure from God.

When did the revelation come? While Paul was on the Damascus Road (Acts 9:1-16) and during his seclusion in Arabia. Thus, his message and the authority to proclaim it depended in no way upon any human source but were totally from Jesus Christ.

Paul's Manner of Life

Paul provided irrefutable historical facts to prove that neither his conversion nor his commission as an apostle could have come through a human channel. First, he reminded the Judaizers of his past religion: "ye have heard of my manner of life in time past in the Jews' religion [Jewish faith]" (v. 13). In Philippians Paul set forth his pedigree as a Jew: ritually, "Circumcised the eighth day"; in relationship, "of the stock of Israel"; in respectability, "of the tribe of Benjamin"; his race, "an Hebrew of the Hebrews"; religiously, "as touching the law, a Pharisee"; in reputation, "Concerning zeal, persecuting the church"; in righteousness, "touching the righteousness which is in the law, blameless" (Phil 3:5-6).[1] There was nothing in Paul's Jewish background to draw him to the salvation in Christ that he now proclaimed and defended, proving that he had no knowledge or instruction in the gospel before his conversion.

Second, Paul persecuted the righteous: "beyond measure I persecuted the church of God, and wasted it" (v. 13). The word *persecute* means *drive away, harass, trouble, put to flight*. Paul was extremely hostile toward Christians and did everything in his power to destroy them. The words *persecuted* and *wasted* are in the imperfect tense and picture the apostle continually trying to exterminate the church before his conversion. He consented to Stephen's death (Acts 8:1), committed men and women to prison (Acts 8:3), breathed out threatenings and slaughter against the disciples (Acts 9:1), and had authority from the high priest to apprehend Christians wherever he found them (Acts 9:1-2; cp. 22:4-5; 26:9-11). Paul was more zealous to destroy the church than any other Jew. Because of this hatred, he saw himself as the chief of sinners (1 Tim. 1:15) and unworthy to be called an apostle (1 Cor. 15:9).

Third, Paul had a passion for religion: "And profited in the Jews' religion above many my equals in mine own nation, being more exceedingly zealous of the traditions of my fathers" (v. 14). The word *profit* speaks of a pioneer advancing by cutting his way through brushwood. Paul blazed the way in his commitment to the Mosaic and Oral Law. The "traditions of my fathers," as Paul put it, were the Oral Law, which he, as a Pharisee, would have kept. Jesus strongly condemned the keeping of the Oral Law by the Pharisees (Mt. 15:1-16; Mk. 7:6-13).

Paul had zealously studied the law at the feet of the great rabbinical teacher Gamaliel (Acts 22:3), advanced further and faster in the Jewish religion than any of his peers, and was destined to become a great rabbinic scholar in his own right. Adding to his personal commitment to Judaism a zeal to please God and his aggressive destruction of the church, Paul would never have left Judaism to become a Christian through the witness or instruction of any man. Only a personal confrontation, such as Paul had, with the risen Christ would have led to his salvation (Acts 9:3-9). No human agent could have changed him from a violent persecutor into a vital preacher of Christ.[2]

Paul's Ministry

Paul's transition from persecutor to preacher came through the grace of God. He verified this by presenting a detailed testimony of his salvation.

First, he was chosen by God: "it pleased God, who separated me from my mother's womb" (v. 15). The word *separated* means *marked off*, referring not to the apostle's physical birth but to specific spiritual service. He had been chosen before his birth—as had Jacob (Rom. 9:11-13), Isaiah (Isa. 49:1), Jeremiah (Jer. 1:5), Samson (Jud. 16:17), and John the Baptist (Lk. 1:15)—to be an apostle to the Gentiles (Acts 9:15; Rom. 11:13).

Second, he was called "by his [God's] grace" (v. 15). The efficacious call to salvation came by means of God's grace through faith and was a pure gift from God, not the result of any work done by Paul; thus, he could not boast in his salvation (Eph. 2:8-9).

Third, this resulted in conversion, for God "reveal[ed] his Son in me" (v. 16), said Paul. He was born again when the Lord appeared to him on the Damascus Road (Acts 9:3-6). The words "in me" should be taken subjectively, referring to the new life of Christ revealed in him that he might become an apostle to the Gentiles.

Fourth, after Paul's conversion he was commissioned to "preach him [Christ] among the Gentiles" (v. 16). Paul was commissioned to take the gospel "unto all men" (Acts 22:15; 26:16-19; cp. 9:15).

Fifth, he did not consult "with flesh and blood [any man]" (v. 16) after his salvation. Although he spent a few days with Ananias, he did not seek advice, understanding, or clarification concerning the revelation he had received from Christ.[3]

Sixth, he had no contact with the Jerusalem church to seek their advice after his Damascus Road experience: "Neither went I up to Jerusalem to them who were apostles before me" (v. 17). Paul had no contact with any Christians *before* his conversion (v. 12) or immediately *after* it, but sought instruction only in the things of Christ.

Seventh, after his salvation he departed from Damascus for another country: "but [on the contrary] I went into Arabia" (v. 17). Paul did not indicate how soon after his salvation he left for Arabia, where he went in that country, how long he stayed, or why he went. Perhaps he left soon after his conversion to receive the needed teachings from Christ, have fellowship with Him, and take time to prepare for his ministry. After a period of time, he "returned again unto Damascus" (v. 17). Possibly Paul preached the gospel in Damascus after his conversion (Acts 9:20-21), went to Arabia, then returned to preach again in the city from which he had fled for his life from those Jews who sought to kill him (Acts 9:23-25). Whatever the case, Paul emphasized that he spent three years in Arabia and Damascus after his salvation, but he never once went to any of the apostles at Jerusalem during this time. One thing is sure: If Paul had wanted to consult with other believers, he would not have waited three years to do so.

Eighth, three years after his salvation Paul sought only companionship with the Jerusalem church: "I went up to Jerusalem to see Peter, and abode with him fifteen days" (v. 18). The apostle was not in Jerusalem for instruction from Peter but only to become acquainted with him. His stay was only 15 days, hardly enough time for any in-depth instruction. Once again, persecution cut short Paul's stay in Jerusalem (Acts 9:29). The Lord appeared to Paul while he was praying in the Temple and ordered him to flee the city for his life (Acts 22:17-18).

Paul made it a point to mention that he saw no other apostle "except James, the Lord's brother" (v. 19), a leader of the Jerusalem church (Acts 12:17). It was Barnabas (*son of consolation*) who befriended Paul and brought him to Peter and James, giving testimony of the apostle's bold preaching in Damascus (Acts 9:27).

Ninth, Paul concluded his testimony with an oath to

God: "Now the things which I write unto you, behold, before God, I lie not" (v. 20). Paul swore an oath to God so that the brethren in Galatia would see the truth of his statements and to confirm that the accusations made by the Judaizers were false.

Paul's Mission

Persecution forced Paul out of Jerusalem after only 15 days in the city. From there he ventured into "the regions of Syria and Cilicia" (v. 21) to minister. He mentioned this area to verify that he was under his own authority, not that of the Jerusalem apostles, for they would never have sent him into such an area to minister.

From there Paul carried on a long ministry until the time he went up to the church council at Jerusalem. It was to Paul's hometown of Tarsus in Cilicia that Barnabas went to fetch Paul for the work in Antioch, the capital of Syria (Acts 11:25-26). From Antioch, Paul was commissioned for his first missionary journey, along with his faithful friend Barnabas (Acts 13:1-3).

Paul was "unknown [lit., *remained unknown*] by face unto the churches of Judæa" (v. 22). He had spent only a few days in Jerusalem, which did not give him time or opportunity to become acquainted with the churches and brethren throughout the region. This is another proof that Paul was not taught by men under the discipleship of any of the Jerusalem church leaders.

After his initial visit to see Peter and James, Paul made only two visits to Jerusalem during the next 14 years, one to bring relief money from Antioch (Acts 11:29-30) and the other to attend the church council (Acts 15).

All that the Judæan churches knew about Paul was that "He who persecuted us in times past now preacheth the faith which once he destroyed" (v. 23). The preaching of "the faith" does not refer to "the body of truth preached by

Paul, but to the faith in Christ which he exhorted his listeners to exercise."[4] Before his conversion, the apostle had tried to destroy (*overthrow continually*) the Christians who had put their faith in Christ.

Paul ended his testimony by saying, "And they glorified God in me" (v. 24). Paul did not say that they rejoiced over his salvation or gloried in him as a trophy of grace, but that they "glorified God" in him. Paul never accepted for himself the glory for what God had done in his life. How different the reaction of the Judaizers, who continually gloried in the flesh.

We must remember the words of Jesus, "Let your light so shine before men, that they may see your good works, and glorify your Father, who is in heaven" (Mt. 5:16). Friend, are others glorifying God because of what Christ has done in your life? Will your testimony stand against the fire of ridicule, false accusations, and persecution?

Paul had silenced the Judaizers' absurd accusations concerning his credentials as an apostle. His testimony was sterling. His call, conversion, and commission had been received without question by the apostles and the church in Jerusalem. Therefore, he warned the Galatian church to close its ears to the voices of dissension that were discrediting him and pay serious attention to his words of admonition, lest they succumb to the legalistic heresy of the Judaizers.

Christians today must be discerning and guard against contemporary Judaizers who skillfully twist the gospel by *adding to* or *taking away from* its truth. In this day of compromise and apostasy, we should all heed Paul's words to the Colossian church: "Beware lest any man spoil you through philosophy and vain deceit, after the tradition of men, after the rudiments of the world, and not after Christ" (Col. 2:8).

ENDNOTES

[1] Lehman Strauss, *Devotional Studies in Philippians* (Neptune, NJ: Loizeaux Brothers, 1959), pp. 149-157.

[2] C. Fred Dickason, Jr., *From Bondage to Freedom, Studies in Galatians* (Chicago: Moody Bible Institute, 1963), part 1, p. 9.

[3] John MacArthur, Jr., *The MacArthur New Testament Commentary*, Galatians (Chicago: Moody Press, 1987), p. 30.

[4] Kenneth S. Wuest, *Wuest's Word Studies from the Greek New Testament*, Galatians (Grand Rapids: Wm. B. Eerdmans Publishing Company, 1944), p. 55.

Then fourteen years after, I went up again to Jerusalem with Barnabas, and took Titus with me also. And I went up by revelation, and communicated unto them that gospel which I preach among the Gentiles, but privately to them who were of reputation, lest by any means I should run, or had run, in vain. But neither Titus, who was with me, being a Greek, was compelled to be circumcised; And that because of false brethren unawares brought in, who came in secretly to spy out our liberty which we have in Christ Jesus, that they might bring us into bondage; To whom we gave place by subjection, no, not for an hour, that the truth of the gospel might continue with you. But of these who seemed to be somewhat (whatever they were, it maketh no matter to me; God accepteth no man's person)—for they who seemed to be somewhat in conference added nothing to me But, on the contrary, when they saw that the gospel of the uncircumcision was committed unto me, as the gospel of the circumcision was unto Peter (For he that wrought effectually in Peter to the apostleship of the circumcision, the same was mighty in me toward the Gentiles)— And when James, Cephas, and John, who seemed to be pillars, perceived the grace that was given unto me, they gave to me and Barnabas the right hands of fellowship, that we should go unto the Gentiles, and they unto the circumcision. Only they would that we should remember the poor; the same which I also was diligent to do (Galatians 2:1-10).

3

A SERVANT APPROVED

"...they gave to me and Barnabas the right hands
of fellowship, that we should go unto
the Gentiles..." (2:9).

Opposition to Paul and his ministry was vicious.
Judaizers had sown seeds of contention throughout Galatia. They had questioned Paul's commission as an
apostle, compromised the gospel by mixing law and grace,
and corrupted local churches with their legalistic preaching. The churches that Paul had established were confused
and in desperate need of direction if they were to survive.

The apostle went up to Jerusalem to counter the opposition of the Judaizers. He hoped that his meeting with the
other apostles would result in approval of his apostolic
authority among the churches, acceptance of his gospel to
the Gentiles, and agreement between himself and the other
apostles on doctrine and practice.

Paul rehearsed the results of his meeting in Jerusalem to establish conclusively his apostolic authority among the churches in Galatia.

Apostles Consulted

Paul returned to Jerusalem 14 years after his previous visit, this time with Barnabas and Titus (v. 1). Most likely this was not the visit made three years after his conversion (1:18) plus 14 years, but the visit that took place 14 years after his conversion. Scholars differ on whether this was the *famine relief* visit from Antioch (Acts 11:27-30) or the visit made during the first church council in Jerusalem around 49 A.D. (Acts 15:1-35). Evidence seems to favor the famine visit from Antioch.

The apostle "went up by revelation" (v. 2), not at the request of any church leader, to confer with the apostles in Jerusalem. How the revelation came to Paul is not mentioned. Some scholars believe it came through Agabus (Acts 11:28), who inspired Paul's famine visit to Jerusalem.

Paul felt no obligation to receive approval for his gospel from the apostles in Jerusalem. He had received that 14 years earlier when Christ revealed the gospel to him. But he wanted to show the church leadership that his gospel to the Gentiles did not require them to be circumcised or to keep any form of the Mosaic Law to be saved.

If the Jerusalem leadership had rejected Paul's gospel, he would have felt like an athlete who had exerted great effort to train for and win a race, only to learn that he "had run, in vain" (v. 2)—that is, to have implemented his ministry among the Gentiles only to have it rejected by the church. But in the apostle's mind, that was not the case. In fact, Paul would have run in vain had he compromised his gospel to include the legalism preached by the Judaizers.

Disapproval by the Jerusalem church would not have invalidated the apostle's ministry, but such division would have created a serious schism between the Jews and Gentiles and the apostles, thus hindering the proclamation of the gospel. Later in this chapter we are told that the apostles did approve of Paul's ministry to the Gentiles.

Paul brought Titus to Jerusalem as a test case to refute the rite of circumcision being propagated by the Judaizers. He said, "neither Titus, who was with me, being a Greek, was compelled to be circumcised" (v. 3). Titus, a Gentile and a true believer, provided irrefutable proof that it was unnecessary for Gentile Christians to keep the Mosaic Law to be saved. Requiring Titus to be circumcised would have been tantamount to denying justification by grace through faith apart from the law.

The later decision by the Jerusalem council not to require Gentile believers to be circumcised sustained Paul's position (Acts 15). Thus, the apostle successfully defended his position of salvation by grace apart from any legalistic requirements put forth by the Judaizers.

Apostates Confronted

Those who would have compelled Titus to be circumcised were labeled by Paul as "false brethren" (v. 4). Although it is not stated, the false brethren were probably Judaizers who taught, "Except ye be circumcised after the manner of Moses, ye cannot be saved" (Acts 15:1).

These individuals were secretly brought into the church "unawares" (v. 4). The concept is of spies who infiltrate the enemy's camp for the purpose of subterfuge and sabotage (cp. 2 Pet. 2:1; Jude 4). Their motive was twofold: First, surveillance—"to spy out" the "liberty" that the apostles had "in Christ Jesus" (v. 4). This liberty freed the apostles from the Mosaic Law with its external ceremonies and ritualism. The basis for their freedom was "in Christ Jesus," whose sacrificial death redeemed mankind from the curse of the law (3:3; 4:5). Second, to make slaves of the

Christians, or "bring [them] into bondage" (v. 4). The word *bondage* has the idea of reducing to abject slavery. The Judaizers wanted to bring Paul and his followers into bondage—first to themselves and then to the Mosaic Law, which would eventually have caused Gentile believers to live a Torah-centered lifestyle and forced a return to enslavement under the law, from which believers had been liberated (3:23-4:11).

Paul and his co-workers did not submit to the Judaizers' demands. He said, "To whom we gave place by subjection, no, not for an hour" (v. 5). Not for one hour would they succumb to the subversive demands of the Judaizers.

What was the reason for taking such a strong stand? "That the truth of the gospel might continue with [for] you" (v. 5)—so that there would be no compromise for the truth found in the gospel, both for the Galatians and for all Christians who would follow.

Several practical lessons can be gleaned from Paul's teaching. First, the Jerusalem church agreed that the Gentiles did not have to keep the law or become Jews to possess salvation (Acts 15:13-21). Second, false brethren and doctrinal error should be dealt with immediately; they should not be allowed to exist in the church. Third, Christians must realize that while Christ has liberated them from the law, this does not give them license to live as they please. Believers are still under the "law of Christ" (6:2). Fourth, Scripture makes it clear that believers should not give heed to false teachers (Eph. 4:14) or their teachings (2 Tim. 4:3-4; Jude 3-4). Those who succumb to such charlatans are partakers of their evil deeds (2 Jn. 10-11). This is fair warning to Christians who listen to media preachers who are in doctrinal error. Christians should not give them one moment of their time.

Authority of Colleagues

Once again Paul focused on his relationship with the leaders in the Jerusalem church. He acknowledged that "James, Cephas, and John...seemed to be pillars" in the church (v. 9). But he also said that "they who seemed to be somewhat in conference added nothing to me" (v. 6). The leadership of the church at Jerusalem did not cause Paul to alter his gospel message to the Gentiles.

It may appear that Paul spoke abusively about the apostolic leadership in Jerusalem, but such was not the case. He was not being disrespectful to them when he said, "whatever they were, it maketh no matter to me" (v. 6). He was merely emphasizing that his authority as an apostle stood independent of those in Jerusalem.

The Lord does not receive people on the basis of appearance: "God accepteth no man's person" (v. 6). Their position in the church did not matter to Paul, for God does not show partiality to people based on leadership or position. The apostle was on the same level as the Jerusalem leadership, for, like them, he had been chosen, called, and commissioned by Christ personally. Therefore, those individuals did not add anything to Paul concerning revelation from the Lord. The Jerusalem apostles did not impose on Paul any burden of doctrine or practice, nor did they impart to him anything in addition to what he already knew.

Apostolic Confirmation

"On the contrary," the apostles received Paul "when they saw that the gospel of the uncircumcision was committed unto" him (v. 7). The word *committed* implies that he was entrusted with a permanent commission to herald the gospel to the Gentiles, "as the gospel of the circumcision was unto Peter" (v. 7). His acceptance by the Jerusalem apostles forever laid to rest the Judaizers' claim that he preached another gospel. In fact, Paul was appointed by the Jerusalem council to take this decision—salvation is by grace apart from any work of the law—to churches in Antioch, Syria, and Cilicia (Acts 15:22-24). It was in those places that the Judaizers had done their greatest damage.

Readers must not assume that verse 7 refers to two different gospels. Paul and the other apostles were in doctrinal unity concerning the content of their gospel (1:6-9), but they employed different missionary strategies in their respective ministries.

The relationship of Paul's commission to the Gentiles and Peter's to the Jews is confirmed by the parenthetical note in verse 8, where the word "he" refers to the enabling power of the Holy Spirit, who commissioned and blessed the ministries of both apostles.

Paul's ministry was formally recognized by "James, Cephas, and John," who extended to him and his co-workers "the right hands of fellowship" (v. 9). This enthusiastic endorsement provided unity within the church and brought sanctions against the Judaizers' position. The Jerusalem apostles did not go only to the Jews, nor did Paul go only to the Gentiles. Scripture teaches that Peter and Paul had overlapping ministries to both Jews and Gentiles (Acts 10:34-48; 13:5, 14ff; 14:1; 16:13, 16; 17:1, 10; 18:4, 19; 19:8).

A number of applications can be made regarding the relationship between the apostles. First, when contention among church leaders arises, it must be settled in an attitude of prayer, allowing the Holy Spirit to direct whatever decisions are made. Second, diverse ministries can complement each other within a fellowship, and they should be acknowledged, provided that the gospel is not compromised. Third, a spirit of competition should not be tolerated within church ministries. Fourth, there should be total cooperation in ministry among people of like faith.

Only one request was made of Paul and Barnabas by the Jerusalem church. They were asked to "remember the poor" (v. 10). This the apostles had done by bringing relief money from Antioch to suffering Judæan believers experiencing a famine (Acts 11:29-30). Most likely poverty was rampant throughout the communities of both Jewish and Gentile believers because of discrimination and persecution. Paul was willing not only to comply with the request, but to be "diligent" (v. 10)—eager to honor such requests throughout his ministry (Rom. 15:25-26; 1 Cor. 16:1-4; 2 Cor. 8:1-6; 9:1-5, 12).

Several practical principles emerged during the confirmation of Paul's ministry that should be implemented in churches today. First, the church must ensure that a doctrinally sound gospel is being preached and taught within the fellowship. It must not proclaim a mixture of law and grace. Second, the church must guard against false brethren who creep into the fellowship and cause division with their heretical or legalistic teachings. Third, church leaders—be they pastors, elders, or deacons—must seek spiritual discernment and wisdom to deal with the aforementioned problems. Fourth, we must remember that although the apostles were in doctrinal unity, they could differ on the presentation of their ministries to various groups without causing strife or division.

The bond of brotherly fellowship is important in the work of Christ. David captured its beauty and blessing when he wrote, "Behold, how good and how pleasant it is for brethren to dwell together in unity!" (Ps. 133:1). May we, like the early church, continue steadfastly in the apostles' doctrine and brotherly fellowship as we proclaim the message of salvation by grace through faith to a lost world. This kind of brotherly unity and love will allow our ministry to continue and attract people to Christ.

But when Peter was come to Antioch, I withstood him to the face, because he was to be blamed. For before certain men came from James, he did eat with the Gentiles; but when they were come, he withdrew and separated himself, fearing them who were of the circumcision. And the other Jews dissembled in like manner with him, insomuch that Barnabas also was carried away with their hypocrisy. But when I saw that they walked not uprightly according to the truth of the gospel, I said unto Peter before them all, If thou, being a Jew, livest after the manner of Gentiles, and not as do the Jews, why compellest thou the Gentiles to live as do the Jews? We who are Jews by nature, and not sinners of the Gentiles, Knowing that a man is not justified by the works of the law, but by the faith of Jesus Christ, even we have believed in Jesus Christ, that we might be justified by the faith of Christ, and not by the works of the law; for by the works of the law shall no flesh be justified. But if, while we seek to be justified by Christ, we ourselves also are found sinners, is therefore Christ the minister of sin? God forbid. For if I build again the things which I destroyed, I make myself a transgressor. For I, through the law, am dead to the law, that I might live unto God. I am crucified with Christ: nevertheless I live; yet not I, but Christ liveth in me; and the life which I now live in the flesh I live by the faith of the Son of God, who loved me and gave himself for me. I do not make void the grace of God; for if righteousness come by the law, then Christ is dead in vain (Galatians 2:11-21).

4

CONFRONTING CHURCH COMPROMISE

**"I do not make void the grace of God;
for if righteousness come by the law,
then Christ is dead in vain" (2:21).**

Confronting a brother face to face concerning compromise is never easy or pleasant, especially if that brother is a co-worker of sterling reputation and character and a highly respected church leader. Such encounters must be handled with extreme sensitivity, directed by spiritual wisdom and the Scriptures, and under the control of the Holy Spirit.

Paul closed this personal section of his letter to the Galatians by relating such an encounter with Peter. In a highly charged public incident, Paul boldly confronted Peter concerning his hypocrisy before the church at Antioch. In so doing, Paul confirmed two principles about his ministry: first, that he had equal authority with the other apostles independently granted to him by the Lord;

and second, that he would strongly oppose the preaching and practice of Mosaic legalism wherever and whenever he found it being taught in the church.

The confrontation apparently took place soon after the Jerusalem apostles had given Paul the "right hands of fellowship" (v. 9). Scholars are divided on whether the incident occurred after the famine visits (Acts 11:29-30) or the Jerusalem Council (Acts 15:3-4).

Peter's Compromise

We are not told why Peter went to Antioch. Possibly it was to visit Paul and see firsthand how the work was progressing. While he was in Antioch, it was Peter's custom to fellowship and eat with Gentiles in the church (v. 12). The imperfect tenses of the verbs indicate that Peter had been doing this for some time on a regular basis; thus, he did not keep *kashrut* (the Jewish dietary laws). But when the Jewish leaders from the church in Jerusalem came to Antioch, Peter "withdrew and separated himself, fearing them who were of the circumcision" (v. 12). Peter gradually segregated himself from Gentiles, fellowshiping and eating only with Jewish believers. Why? Because he feared being criticized by his Jewish brethren. Peter's actions caused the other Jewish believers in the church to join in the hypocrisy—even Barnabas (v. 13).

Paul called Peter's compromise what it really was— "hypocrisy" (v. 13). The word *hypocrisy* was used in the Greek theater to describe actors who put large painted masks in front of their faces to denote the characters they were playing, thus hiding their real identities. Today the term is used to describe a deceitful or two-faced person. Peter was being two-faced, pretending that his actions were motivated by faithfulness to the Lord when, in reality, they were motivated by fear of criticism by the Jewish leaders who had come from the Jerusalem church.[1]

Paul's Confrontation

When Paul witnessed Jewish believers not walking "uprightly according to the truth of the gospel" (v. 14), he "withstood [Peter] to the face" (v. 11). Paul condemned Peter's action, "because he was to be blamed [stood condemned]" (v. 11).

The apostle put his rebuke in the form of a question: "If thou, being a Jew, livest after the manner of Gentiles, and not as do the Jews, why compellest thou the Gentiles to live as do the Jews?" (v. 14).

Peter had declared to the Jerusalem council that Gentiles should not be put under the yoke of the law (Acts 15:9-10), but now, by his actions, he had compromised his own convictions. Paul formed his question in such a way that if Peter had tried to answer, he would have admitted his guilt before the whole church. If Paul had not confronted Peter in this manner, liberty in Christ would have been severely eroded, opening the door for Judaizers to corrupt the church.

Paul's Conviction

The apostle seemed to pause after confronting Peter with his question to see if an answer would be forthcoming. But no answer was given, or at least none is recorded. Paul then continued his argument, dealing with three areas of controversy that Peter's compromise had brought into question: the law's relationship to salvation (vv. 15-16); the believers' relationship to the law (vv. 17-19); and the believers' relationship to Christ (vv. 20-21). In these verses, Paul presented an introduction to the theme of his letter, which he developed more thoroughly in chapters 3 and 4.

Paul began his argument with the commonly held Jewish belief that "Jews by nature [birth]" are "not sinners of the Gentiles" (v. 15). Jews were given the law from birth and sought righteousness through it. This set them apart from the

Gentiles, whom the Jews considered to be sinners. This concept does not imply personal immorality committed by individual Gentiles but speaks of their legal standing before God.

Although Jews possessed the law, which was of great advantage to them, they were not justified before God by keeping it, for "a man is not justified by the works of the law, but by [through] the faith [belief] of [in] Jesus Christ" (v. 16). Therefore, a person's justification does not depend on his or her possession of the law; salvation can be obtained only through faith in Christ. Paul emphasized this point. He used the verb form of *justification* four times in verses 16 and 17 and the noun form one time (translated "righteousness") in verse 21.

Paul used the word *justification* in a legal sense, indicating a judicial act of God whereby He justly declares and treats as righteous guilty, condemned sinners who put their faith in Jesus Christ for salvation. Being declared justified before God implies an act of personal commitment, not just a mental assent to facts concerning Christ's sacrificial work on the cross. This is what Paul meant by the statement, "even we have believed in [into] Jesus Christ" (v. 16). People who have been justified are declared righteous by God and are devoid of condemnation for past transgressions (Rom. 8:1, 31-34). Three times in this verse Paul reminded Jewish believers that they were not justified "by the works of the law" (v. 16) but by faith or belief in Jesus Christ (cp. Rom. 3:19-28).

Paul went on to show the absurdity of Peter's action by raising a hypothetical question that Judaizers might make against his argument. He asked, "But if, while we seek to be justified by Christ, we ourselves also are found sinners, is therefore Christ the minister of sin?" (v. 17). Scholars differ over the exact meaning of this difficult verse. The best way to interpret the verse seems to be: (1) You say that salvation comes through faith in Christ alone, apart from any aspects of the Mosaic Law. (2) As believers, you are free from law-keeping. (3) If the law is done away with in Christ, you have no way to govern the way you should live as a Christian. (4) Paul's lawless theology in Christ has brought you to a lifestyle that is no better than that of Gentile sinners. (5) Thus, a doctrine of justification by Christ alone is an incentive to live a life of sin. (6) Hence, Christ is responsible for your moral failure. (7) Therefore, Christ is the minister of sin.[2]

We can only imagine the embarrassment and awkward position in which Paul put Peter and Barnabas. The apostle had called them hypocrites and sinners and claimed that their practice of law-keeping played right into the position of the Judaizers. But to his hypothetical question, Paul quickly proclaimed, "God forbid" (v. 17), or *Perish the thought!* As painful as it was for Paul to raise such a difficult question, he had to do it to make a strong case against the hypocritical practice of Peter and the others.

To soften his rebuke of Peter, Paul changed the "we" (vv. 16-17) to "I" (v. 18), thus using himself in a hypothetical situation (although still referring to Peter). He said, "For if I build again the things which I destroyed, I make myself a transgressor" (v. 18). If Paul returned to the Mosaic Law after he had believed and preached that justification before God could be appropriated only through faith in Christ, he would be rebuilding that which he had destroyed. Thus, by leaving grace and returning to the law, he would become a hypocrite (a "transgressor," v. 18).[3]

Jewish believers in this generation must guard against keeping certain legalistic teachings found in Rabbinical Judaism, thus giving the impression that they are mixing law with the grace of Christ. Neither should Gentile believers feel that they have missed out on some special blessing by not keeping the laws of the Old Testament or Rabbinical Judaism, for believers are complete in Christ (Col. 2:9-10).

Paul's Comparison

To make his case stronger, Paul related his own experience with the law. He said, "For I, through the law, am dead to the law, that I might live unto God" (v. 19). The apostle had found that keeping the law could never give him life, for no one could fulfill its demands for righteousness. The law, said Paul, revealed sin, provoked sin, provided no remedy for sin, and actually condemned him. Therefore, he left the law as a means to become just before God and put his faith in Christ as the means by which he was declared righteous. This meant that Paul was "dead to the law" and free from its claims, relationship, or control over his life.[4]

This was no imaginary or self-imposed death but a real, imputed death with Christ. When Christ bore the believers' sins, He died under the just demands of the law (3:13), forever breaking the believers' relationship to it (Rom. 7:4). Thus, Paul was alive unto God (v. 19), bringing him into a new and living relationship with Him.

In verse 20 Paul repeated this idea, but in greater detail. He said, "I am [have been] crucified with Christ: nevertheless I live." The word *crucified* is in the perfect tense, emphasizing both the past act of Christ's crucifixion and its continuing, present, finished result. Dr. Kenneth Wuest provides a good explanation of what Paul meant by believers being crucified with Christ. He writes,

> Paul uses it to show that his identification with Christ at the Cross was a past fact, and that the spiritual benefits that have come to him through his identification are present realities with him. By this statement he also shows how he died to the law, namely by dying with Christ who died under its penalty. The law's demands were satisfied and therefore have no more hold on Paul. But thus being crucified with Christ, meant also to

> Paul, death to self. When Paul died with Christ, it was the Pharisee Saul who died. What he was and did up to that time passed away so far as he was concerned. Saul was buried, and the old life with him. The dominating control of the Adamic nature had its power over him broken.[5]

In another place Wuest identified the *old life* (unregenerate man), often called the *old man*. "The old man here refers to that person the believer was before he was saved, totally depraved, unregenerate, lacking the life of God."[6] It should be made clear that when Dr. Wuest speaks of the *person* dying, he is referring to the unregenerate man or the person in his or her unregenerate state, and not the individual's *old disposition*, often called the *old nature*.

Dr. Renald E. Showers, in his book, *The New Nature*, provides a convincing argument for believing that it is the person in his or her unregenerate state that has died, and not the person's disposition or nature. He writes,

> Firstly, the whole context of Romans 6:1-13 talks about persons, not dispositions, having died. In Romans 6:2, 8 Paul says that "we" died; in verse 7 he says that "he" died. A disposition is only one aspect of a person; it cannot be said that in reality it is a person.

> Secondly, in Romans 6:7 Paul draws a distinction between the person who died and the sinful disposition. He declares that the person who died is freed from the sinful disposition. He thereby makes it clear that it is the person, not the disposition that died.

> Thirdly, the view that says that it is the sinful disposition that died with Christ distorts the concept or identification with Christ's death

taught in this passage. When Christ died it was a person, not just a disposition, that died. Christ became a human being so that He could die as the substitute for human persons, not as the substitute for a sinful disposition.

Fourthly, when Paul applies his teaching (Romans 6:11), he exhorts Christians to reckon *themselves* to be dead. He does not tell them to reckon their sinful dispositions to be dead. Certainly Paul would have exhorted the latter if their dispositions had been crucified.

Fifthly, in Romans 6:2, 11 Paul declares that the believer has died to sin. He does not say that sin has died to the believer.

Sixthly, if the sinful disposition has been crucified with Christ, then that disposition is dead in the Christian. This would mean that the Christian has no struggle with sin. But Romans 7:14-25 indicates that the Christian does have a struggle with sin. In fact, Romans 7:14-25 and Galatians 5 teach that the sinful disposition is very much alive and active in the Christian.

Seventhly, in...Galatians 2:20 Paul declares that it was he who was crucified with Christ. He does not say that his sinful disposition was crucified.

It should be concluded, then, that *the "old man" is that unregenerate man or the human person in his unregenerate state.* As an old man, the unsaved person holds the position of slave under his sinful disposition.

In light of this meaning of "old man," when Paul says that our old man was crucified with Christ, he is teaching that there is some sense in which the unregenerate person actually dies when he becomes a Christian.[7]

Thus, Paul had been brought to a new legal union through faith in Christ. When he accepted the Lord, he became dead to the old life (man) and was resurrected to newness of life as the living Christ indwelt him (cp. 3:27; Rom. 6:3-11; 1 Cor. 12:13). Therefore, Paul could say, "yet not I, but Christ liveth in me" (v. 20).

Paul went on to say, "and the life which I now live in the flesh I live by the faith of the Son of God, who loved me and gave himself for me" (v. 20). Although he had a new life in the flesh, he was not motivated by the flesh but by faith in Christ. Thus, it is faith in Christ and not works (legal obedience) that releases divine power to live out the Christian life.[8] Paul's faith was anchored in the work of Christ, who, in unselfish and sacrificial love, "gave himself" (v. 20) through crucifixion for the sins of the world (cp. 1:4).

Paul concluded his argument against Peter and the others by showing that the hypocrisy of law-keeping made "void [nullified or set aside] the grace of God; for if righteousness come by the law, then Christ is dead in vain" (v. 21). That would make His death unnecessary, a useless tragedy, the greatest travesty in human history—a conclusion that was unthinkable and blasphemous in its ramifications. To many, Peter's act might seem harmless—a little thing not worth making a fuss over, let alone being considered a compromise. But it was more than a little thing or mere compromise; it was hypocrisy, as Paul rightly called it.

Few people would boldly confront a leader of Peter's stature and call him a hypocrite, as Paul did. Most leaders do not confront their peers but, rather, insulate or isolate themselves, remaining uninvolved. The attitude today is, *Don't rock the boat. Live and let live.* In this way, compromising practices can creep into churches and mission organizations, leading them into unsound doctrinal positions and practices.

A number of lessons can be learned from the effects of Peter's hypocrisy on Christians and the church. First, he led into hypocrisy some who followed him as a leader (such as Barnabas). Second, his actions taught that there was a distinction between Jewish and Gentile believers, when none existed. Third, he sent a message to the Christian community that Jewish believers must keep the law, which was untrue. Fourth, Peter's conduct destroyed unity within the church, bringing about division in the fellowship. Fifth, his compromise was a clear example that gifted ministers with a position of authority and responsibility can go astray. Sixth, faithfulness is more than believing right doctrine; it must be lived out in correct practice. Seventh, Peter was practicing situation ethics, which is not biblical. Eighth, compromise provides opportunity for heretical teaching to invade the church.

Remember, compromise must be confronted if the church is to remain healthy and on a sound foundation.

ENDNOTES

[1] Warren W. Wiersbe, *The Bible Exposition Commentary*, Galatians (Wheaton: Victor Books, Vol. I, 1989), p. 694.

[2] Richard N. Longenecker, *Word Biblical Commentary*, Galatians (Dallas: Word Books, 1990), p. 89.

[3] John Mac Arthur, *The MacArthur New Testament Commentary*, Galatians (Chicago: Moody Press, 1987), pp. 58-59.

[4] Kenneth S. Wuest, *Wuest's Word Studies*, Galatians (Grand Rapids: Wm. B. Eerdmans Publishing Co., 1944), p. 80.

[5] *Op. Cit.*, Wuest, p. 81.

[6] *Op. Cit.*, Wuest, Romans, p. 101.

[7] Renald E. Showers, *The New Nature* (Neptune, NJ: Loizeaux Brothers, 1986), pp. 65-67.

[8] Donald K. Campbell, *The Bible Knowledge Commentary*, Galatians (Wheaton: Victor Books, 1983), Vol. II, p. 596.

O foolish Galatians, who hath bewitched you, that ye should not obey the truth, before whose eyes Jesus Christ hath been openly set forth, crucified among you? This only would I learn of you, Received ye the Spirit by the works of the law, or by the hearing of faith? Are ye so foolish? Having begun in the Spirit, are ye now made perfect by the flesh? Have ye suffered so many things in vain?—if it be yet in vain. He, therefore, that ministereth to you the Spirit, and worketh miracles among you, doeth he it by the works of the law, or by the hearing of faith? Even as Abraham believed God, and it was accounted to him for righteousness. Know ye, therefore, that they who are of faith, the same are the sons of Abraham. And the scripture, foreseeing that God would justify the Gentiles through faith, preached before the gospel unto Abraham, saying, In thee shall all nations be blessed. So, then, they who are of faith are blessed with faithful Abraham. For as many as are of the works of the law are under the curse; for it is written, Cursed is everyone that continueth not in all things which are written in the book of the law, to do them. But that no man is justified by the law in the sight of God, it is evident; for, The just shall live by faith. And the law is not of faith, but, The man that doeth them shall live in them. Christ hath redeemed us from the curse of the law, being made a curse for us; for it is written, Cursed is everyone that hangeth on a tree; That the blessing of Abraham might come on the Gentiles through Jesus Christ, that we might receive the promise of the Spirit through faith (Galatians 3:1-14).

5

JUSTIFIED BY FAITH ALONE

**"...no man is justified by the law in the sight of God,
it is evident; for,
The just shall live by faith" (3:11).**

Dr. William Culbertson, former President of Moody Bible Institute, often concluded his prayer with the words, "Lord, I pray that we will finish well." He realized that many people begin their Christian walk well but do not finish well. They are driven off course by false doctrine, legalistic teaching, or worldly entanglements that take them far afield from their original commitment.

Problems like these plagued the Galatian church. Although many Galatians had trusted Christ for their salvation, they had fallen prey to the Judaizers, who added law-keeping as a prerequisite for salvation. Such beliefs could not be tolerated, for to supplement the work of Christ with the works of the law was to replace it. In chapters 3 and 4 of his epistle to the Galatians, Paul argued that justification and sanctification come through faith in Christ alone, apart from any legalistic requirements.[1]

Principle of Faith Without the Law

Strongly condemning these believers for their departure from the faith, the apostle called them "foolish Galatians" (v. 1). The word *foolish* means *thoughtless, unreflective,* or *lacking in spiritual discernment.* The Galatians were being irrational and exhibiting a lack of spiritual discernment by embracing a doctrinal position that made Christ's death of no effect (cp. 2:21).

By asking six rhetorical questions, the apostle tried to awaken the Galatians to their spiritual condition. First, he showed surprise at their falling away: "Who hath bewitched you, that ye should not obey the truth...?" (v. 1). The word *bewitched* has the idea of *casting an evil eye* on someone through a mysterious spell. Paul was amazed that the Galatians had allowed the Judaizers to draw them away with demonic teaching, when "before [their] eyes Jesus Christ hath been openly set forth [as on a public placard], crucified among [them]" (v. 1). Their eyes had beheld the truth in Christ, but now they were being blinded to that truth, as if mesmerized by the Judaizers' legalistic teachings. The apostle was bewildered and dumbfounded that the Galatians had allowed this to occur.

Second, he asked how they had received the Holy Spirit: "Received ye the Spirit by the works of the law, or by the hearing of faith?" (v. 2). It was clear that they had received the Holy Spirit by the hearing of faith, for it was through the Holy Spirit that they had been convicted of sin (Jn. 16:8), regenerated (Jn. 3:6-8), baptized into the body of Christ (1 Cor. 12:13), indwelt (Jn. 14:17), sealed (Eph. 1:13), and filled (Eph. 5:18) the moment they put their faith in Christ. No works were involved.

Third, the apostle again reminded them of their stupidity by asking, "Are ye so foolish" (v. 3), or spiritually dull, to believe that you can be saved by grace through faith and then be sanctified by keeping the law? Obviously they were.

Fourth, he questioned their sanctification: "Having begun in the Spirit, are ye now made perfect by the flesh?" (v. 3). They believed that spiritual maturity could be acquired by law-keeping. Again, such thinking lacked spiritual discernment.

Fifth, Paul asked about their personal suffering for the sake of the gospel: "Have ye suffered so many things in vain?" (v. 4). The apostle may have been referring to suffering at the hands of unbelieving Jews (cp. Acts 14:19, 22). By forsaking the principle of grace for law-keeping, the Galatian believers were admitting that their former position was erroneous. Thus, all their suffering was for naught: "if it be yet in vain" (v. 4). But Paul was not willing to concede that they had been won over to the Judaizers' position.

The apostle's sixth question dealt with his supernatural ministry: "He, therefore, that ministereth to you the Spirit, and worketh miracles among you, doeth he it by the works of the law, or by the hearing of faith?" (v. 5). Paul's ministry was confirmed by a number of miracles in Galatia (Acts 14:3, 8-11). This miracle-working power came from God the Father by means of the Holy Spirit and was received through faith, rather than through any human effort or keeping of the Jewish law.

By asking these very pointed questions, the apostle hoped to steer the Galatians back on track in their beliefs as he proved that the gospel had been confirmed among them by grace through faith, rather than through the works of the law.

There are many 20th-century Judaizers who foster a works-righteousness religious system among undiscerning believers. They are taken in by crafty tactics, believing that their salvation and sanctification are not complete unless they follow certain legalistic requirements. Christians must be vigilant and guard against deceivers. The Bible calls those who follow such teachings "foolish."

Progenitor of Faith Before the Law

Judaizers prided themselves on two facts. First, they were children of God through Abraham, circumcised and therefore partakers of the covenant blessings (see Gen. 12; 15; 17).

Second, they kept the law of Moses. But Paul used these teachings to destroy their position. By quoting six Old Testament passages, the apostle proved that Abraham was the progenitor of grace through faith before the law was ever given.

Paul first quoted Genesis 15:6, which showed that Abraham's acceptance before God was purely by faith: "Abraham believed God , and it was accounted to him for righteousness" (v. 6). Abraham's belief in God was a commitment of faith and was imputed to him for righteousness (acceptability before God), apart from any meritorious work (see Rom. 4:1-11).

Linking Abraham's past with the present, Paul applied this fact to those who would follow in the faith of the patriarch: "Know ye, therefore, that they who are of faith, the same are the sons of Abraham" (v. 7). They should have perceived that the true sons of Abraham were not those who were circumcised, but those who exercised faith unto salvation like that of Abraham. The phrase *sons of Abraham* does not mean, as some teach, that Gentiles become spiritual Jews. It refers to Abraham's spiritual heritage as the father of faith, rather than to his physical lineage.

God's original plan anticipated the need for Gentiles to be justified through faith, like Abraham. Paul therefore quoted a second Old Testament passage, Genesis 12:3. "And the scripture, foreseeing that God would justify the Gentiles through faith, preached before the gospel unto Abraham, saying, In thee shall all nations be blessed" (v. 8; cp. Jn. 8:56). This truth was revealed to Abraham before his circumcision, destroying the Judaizers' position that Gentiles had to be circumcised to be saved.

Paul brought his argument to an inescapable affirmation: "So, then, they who are of faith are blessed with faithful Abraham" (v. 9). Physical lineage to the Jewish people or their religion does not tie Gentiles into the spiritual blessings of Abraham; it is faith alone (see Rom. 2:28-29).

People Not Free Under the Law

The Judaizers believed that those who kept the law would receive blessing and approval from God. The apostle marshaled a direct attack against that position by showing that the law brought the opposite results—a curse and condemnation. Quoting from a third Old Testament passage, Deuteronomy 27:26, the Apostle said, "For as many as are of the works of the law are under the curse; for it is written, Cursed is everyone that continueth not in all things which are written in the book of the law, to do them" (v. 10; cp. Jas. 2:10). Failure to keep one small point of the law meant failure in all areas and brought condemnation. The conclusion "is evident," said Paul: "no man is justified by the law in the sight of God" (v. 11).

The apostle confirmed his position by citing a fourth Old Testament passage, Habakkuk 2:4, which linked faith with justification: "For, The just shall live by faith" (v. 11; cp. Rom. 1:17). The word *just* refers to a person who has been justified by God. God declares and treats as righteous people who put their faith in the redemptive work of Christ and lays no charge against them (Rom. 8:1, 31-34).

The writer to the Hebrews quoted Habakkuk 2:4 to show that people who have been justified will live by faith (Heb. 10:38). In this context, many professing believers were considering a return to Judaism because of persecution. The writer to the Hebrews tried to fortify them for future trials by reminding them that they had originally exercised faith in Jesus as their Messiah. He encouraged them not to cast away their confidence in the Lord, for He would richly reward them if they remained true to the faith. In like manner, Paul admonished the Galatian believers to remain true to the faith.

There were others who maintained that because "the law is holy...and just, and good" (Rom. 7:12), it could in some way work together with the faith principle in a Christian's life. By citing a fifth Old Testament passage, Leviticus 18:5, the apostle repudiated this idea by showing that faith and law are mutually exclusive concepts and cannot be mingled together: "And the law is not of faith, but, The man that doeth them shall live in them" (v. 12). In other words, "The Law said, Do and live! but grace says, Believe and live!"[2]

Price of Freedom From the Law

The only hope of being redeemed from the law's curse is through the Savior's redemptive work. Quoting from a sixth Old Testament passage, Deuteronomy 21:23, the apostle said, "Christ hath redeemed us from the curse of the law, being made a curse for us; for it is written, Cursed is everyone that hangeth on a tree" (v. 13). Under the law, a condemned criminal was stoned to death and then tied to a pole for everyone to see that God's justice had been carried out according to the requirements of the law. This is a vivid picture of the ransom paid through Christ's substitutionary death on the cross. The sinless Christ was made sin for mankind (2 Cor. 5:21; cp. 1 Pet. 3:18) when God the Father laid the curse on Him (Isa. 53:6, 10), which He willingly bore (Gal. 1:4; 2:20).[3] He was not personally cursed but was "made" or "became" a curse in place of sinners.

Jesus was hung on a tree (the cross) to show the world that the law's curse had fallen on Him. "Thus, having violated the Law in one part—through no fault of His own—He became technically guilty of all of it and bore the punishment of God's wrath for every violation of the Law by every man."[4] The preposition *for* (*huper*, v. 13) means *over* or *in the place of* (i.e., Christ comes *over* or *between* us and the curse, showing the substitutionary character of His death).

The price for mankind's salvation was paid by Jesus, who has "redeemed us" (v. 13) from the law's curse. The word *redeem* means *to buy out of slavery* by paying the ransom price. Christ's death satisfied the legal demand of the law, making it possible for mankind to be freed from its curse. By receiving Jesus as Savior, both Jews and Gentiles are freed from the law's curse and declared righteous before God (Rom. 3:21-22).

Paul concluded this portion of his argument by giving two purposes for Christ's becoming a curse for us. The first was "That the blessing of Abraham might come on the Gentiles through Jesus Christ" (v. 14). The blessing of Abraham was justification by faith (vv. 8-9). When Christ took the curse upon

Himself, the blessing of salvation flowed to all people, especially the Gentiles who, like Abraham, could be justified by faith. Thus, the middle wall of partition (the law), which kept Jews and Gentiles separated, was done away with in Christ (see Eph. 2:14-18), making it possible for both groups to receive the same spiritual blessing.

The second purpose was "that we might receive the promise of the Spirit through faith" (v. 14). The Spirit had been promised by the Lord before His death (Jn. 14:16-17) and after His resurrection (Lk. 24:49; Acts 1:4). The Holy Spirit's indwelling presence was evidence that people had become believers by grace through faith in Jesus Christ and gave them access to spiritual blessings from God, such as those possessed by Abraham. Thus, salvation and sanctification can be acquired only by grace through faith, not through the works of the law.

Dr. Warren Wiersbe provided a succinct summation of Paul's argument when he wrote, "For the Christian to abandon faith and grace for Law and works is to lose everything exciting that the Christian can experience in his daily fellowship with the Lord. The Law cannot justify the sinner...neither...give him righteousness. The Law cannot give the gift of the Spirit, nor...guarantee that spiritual inheritance that belongs to God's children. The Law cannot give life, and...liberty....Why, then, go back into the Law?"[5]

Let us take to heart Dr. Culbertson's prayer and "finish well."

ENDNOTES

[1] Donald K. Campbell, *The Bible Knowledge Commentary*, Galatians (Wheaton: Victor Books, 1983), Vol. II, p. 596.

[2] Warren W. Wiersbe, *The Bible Exposition Commentary*, Galatians (Wheaton: Victor Books, 1989), Vol. I, p. 699.

[3] C. Fred Dickason, Jr., *From Bondage to Freedom: Studies in Galatians* (Chicago: Moody Bible Institute, 1963), part 1, p. 26.

[4] James Montgomery Boice, *The Expositor's Bible Commentary*, Galatians (Grand Rapids: Zondervan Publishing House, 1976), Vol. X, p. 460.

[5] Wiersbe, *op. cit.*, p. 700.

Brethren, I speak after the manner of men: Though it be but a man's covenant, yet if it be confirmed, no man annulleth or addeth to it. Now to Abraham and his seed were the promises made. He saith not, And to seeds, as of many; but as of one, And to thy seed, which is Christ. And this I say, that the covenant that was confirmed before by God in Christ, the law, which was four hundred and thirty years after, cannot annul, that it should make the promise of no effect. For if the inheritance be of the law, it is no more of promise; but God gave it to Abraham by promise. Wherefore, then, serveth the law? It was added because of transgressions, till the seed should come to whom the promise was made; and it was ordained by angels in the hand of a mediator. Now a mediator is not a mediator of one, but God is one. Is the law, then, against the promises of God? God forbid; for if there had been a law given which could have given life, verily righteousness should have been by the law. But the scripture hath concluded all under sin, that the promise by faith of Jesus Christ might be given to them that believe. But before faith came, we were kept under the law, shut up unto the faith which should afterwards be revealed. Wherefore, the law was our schoolmaster to bring us unto Christ, that we might be justified by faith. But after faith is come, we are no longer under a schoolmaster. For ye are all the sons of God by faith in Christ Jesus. For as many of you as have been baptized into Christ have put on Christ. There is neither Jew nor Greek, there is neither bond nor free, there is neither male nor female; for ye are all one in Christ Jesus. And if ye be Christ's, then are ye Abraham's seed, and heirs according to the promise (Galatians 3:15-29).

6

ONCE FOR ALL SET FREE

**"...the law was our schoolmaster
to bring us unto Christ,
that we might be justified by faith" (3:24).**

Earlier in Galatians chapter 3, Paul demonstrated that Abraham was justified by faith centuries before the law was given. In like manner, everyone who follows in the faith of Abraham—Jewish or Gentile—is declared justified without the law. In verses 9 to 14 of chapter 3, the apostle skillfully quoted six Old Testament passages to confirm his position.

The Judaizers could have conceded that Abraham was justified by faith alone. But they also might counter Paul's argument with three of their own. First, God gave the Mosaic Law to Israel and, in so doing, changed the means by which salvation is acquired. Second, if salvation is acquired without the law, why was it given? Third, if the law had been set aside, as Paul claimed, it was not valid for him to quote Old Testament passages to prove that the Judaizers' teaching was in error.[1]

Anticipating such objections, Paul proceeded to prove that justification by grace through faith, promised in the Abrahamic Covenant, was permanent and took priority over the Mosaic Law.

Promised Freedom From the Law

The word "Brethren" (v. 15) indicates that Paul had become more conciliatory in his tone to the Galatians. In an attitude of love, he tried to show these misguided people the correctness of his position. The apostle's statement, "I speak after the manner of men" (v. 15), did not mean that his forthcoming argument was less inspired or less authoritative. Simply put, he used "an example from everyday life" (NIV) to make his point.

First, Paul stated that covenants that are confirmed on a human level are not changeable: "Though it be but a man's covenant, yet if it be confirmed, no man annlleth or addeth to it" (v. 15). A covenant ratified by two people on a human level, if it is to remain in effect, cannot be altered in any way by a third party without the permission of the two original parties. In like manner, neither can God's covenant with Abraham be altered. This covenant was more binding than a human agreement because Abraham was in a deep sleep and played no role in it (Gen. 15:12).

Second, arguing from a historical perspective, the apostle showed that promises made to Abraham found their ultimate culmination in "his seed...which is Christ" (v. 16). Paul mentioned "seed," not "seeds" (v. 16), indicating that God made the covenant promise with Abraham through Christ. Therefore, the Mosaic Law cannot alter this covenant.

Third, the law could not cancel the covenant of promise made centuries before the Mosaic Law was given, for "the law, which was four hundred and thirty years after, cannot annul, that it should make the promise of no effect" (v. 17). Paul's reference to 430 years, rather than 400 years (Gen. 15:13), takes into account the time that elapsed between when the Abrahamic Covenant was confirmed through Jacob and the Mosaic Covenant was given at Mount Sinai (cp. Gen. 46:2-4 with Ex. 19:1-2). Therefore, the law, given hundreds of years later, had no impact on the covenant that God made with Abraham.

Fourth, promise and law cannot be combined: "For if the inheritance be of the law, it is no more of promise; but God gave it to Abraham by promise" (v. 18). Promise and law are two opposing principles. Adding any form of the law to the promise would make it void; therefore, justification by faith comes by promise, not by law. God "gave" it that way (v. 18). The word *gave (charizomai)* comes from the same Greek root as the word *grace (charis)*, denoting that the promised inheritance (justification by faith) was given as a free act of God's love long before the law was given. The word appears in the perfect tense, indicating that God gave the inheritance to Abraham in the past, but the inheritance has a present and permanent application for everyone who believes. Moreover, an inheritance is never earned; it is always freely given. Hence the Judaizers' teaching that the law must be kept to obtain the inheritance was in error.

Dr. Kenneth Wuest provides a perceptive note concerning the Judaizers' position: "The doctrine of the Judaizers at first glance appeared only to add some harmless new conditions to the covenant of grace. But the character of these new conditions virtually annulled it. Works added to faith would annul the entire covenant (of promise) since any dependence upon works means that it is necessary to abandon faith."[2]

Primary Focus of the Law
Paul continued his argument by asking the logical

rhetorical question, "Wherefore, then, serveth the law?" (v. 19). That is, Why was the law added? First, "It was added because of transgressions" (v. 19). The word *added* has the idea of being *placed alongside* the covenant of promise, meaning that the law was supplementary and subordinate to it and in no way added conditions for salvation.[3] The law's purpose was to reveal sin as a transgression. Instead of providing righteousness for sinners, the law magnified sin's guilt and made people aware that they could not be saved by keeping the law. Thus, the law could not in any way change the permanent provisions of the covenant.

Second, the law was to be temporary: "It was added...till the seed should come to whom the promise was made" (v. 19). After Christ's crucifixion and resurrection, the law was abrogated, but the covenant of promise remained.

Third, God made the covenant of promise with Abraham directly, but the Mosaic Law "was ordained by angels in the hand of a mediator" (v. 19). The law came through a third party; God gave it to angels, who gave it to Moses, who in turn gave it to Israel. Thus, numerous parties mediated the law, whereas the covenant of promise had no mediator because "God [who] is one" (v. 20) confirmed it by Himself (cp. Gen. 15:12-17). Therefore, the covenant of promise is superior to the Mosaic Law.

This engendered another question in the minds of the Judaizers—a question that Paul had already anticipated: "Is the law, then, against [contrary to or in conflict with] the promises of God?" (v. 21). The apostle's answer was swift and succinct: "God forbid" (v. 21), or perish the thought. Law and promise are not in conflict; they have distinct functions and purposes.

The law was never designed to provide salvation for mankind. Paul said, "if there had been a law given which could have given life, verily righteousness should have been by the law" (v. 21). If this were the case—that the covenant of promise would no longer be in effect—God's grace played no role in salvation and Christ's death was meaningless because it had no power to save anyone. Yet this was not the case because life came by the covenant of promise through Christ rather than through the law. In fact, the opposite is true. Rather than giving life to mankind, the law "concluded [shut up or confined] all under sin" (v. 22). The law imprisoned everyone under its curse and condemnation (cp. Rom. 3:9, 19-20, 23; 7:9-14). However, the law had a greater purpose than to condemn people; it locked them up to "faith of [in] Jesus Christ" (v. 22) as the only means by which the promise of salvation might be granted to them (cp. Rom. 7:24-25).

Paul clearly indicated that law and grace are not in conflict with each other; they simply have different functions. As one writer aptly stated, "The Law is not the basis of God's judgment of men. A sinner who rejects Christ, goes to the Lake of Fire for all eternity, not because he has broken God's laws, for his sin is paid for. He goes to a lost eternity, because he rejects God's grace in the Lord Jesus. The Law is a revelation of the sinner's legal standing, and as such condemns him. It cannot therefore justify him, as the Judaizers claim."[4]

Pedagogical Function of the Law

The apostle continued to counter the Judaizers by illustrating the true function of the law. First, it functioned as a prison: "But before faith came, we were kept under the law, shut up unto the faith which should afterwards be revealed" (v. 23). The phrase *before faith* refers to the Christian faith. Before the Christian faith came, the law held Israel together as a nation and, for most of its history, kept the people from embracing the wicked religions of their neighbors. But when the Christian faith came, the law was abrogated, and spiritual life and liberation were provided for everyone who put their faith in Jesus the Messiah. True, those under the law who exercised faith in God, like father Abraham (Rom. 4:6-8), would be saved. But the law played no part in their salvation.

Second, the law functioned as a pedagogue, for "the law was our schoolmaster to bring us unto Christ, that we might be justified by faith" (v. 24). The word *schoolmaster* does not provide a proper concept of the Greek word *paidagogos*, which means a *child custodian* or *disciplinarian*. The pedagogue was a slave, not a teacher, who governed children aged 6 to 16 for wealthy Greek and Roman households. The pedagogue's function was to take the children to school, correct their moral behavior, protect them from harm, and prepare them for adulthood. In like manner, the law functioned as a temporary custodian restricting sinful mankind under its provisions, so that only through Christ could people "be justified by faith."

The conclusion of Paul's argument is self-evident: "But after faith is come, we are no longer under a schoolmaster" (v. 25). The law no longer has jurisdiction to govern people's lives. They could no longer argue that circumcision, dietary laws, a distinctly Jewish ethical precept, or any other aspect of the Jewish lifestyle were prerequisites for salvation.[5]

Although most Christians would oppose legalism, some churches and individuals, through misinterpretation of Scripture, impose legalistic requirements upon people for their salvation. In reality, they are recapitulating the Judaizers' error. We must continually remember that people are justified by faith in Christ alone.

Positionally Free from the Law

Because believers are no longer under the law but under grace, Paul mentioned four privileges that they enjoy. The first is sonship: "For ye are all the sons of God by faith in Christ Jesus" (v. 26). The apostle's switch from the first person "we" to the second person "ye" indicates a shift of attention from Israel to believers, both Jewish and Gentile. Believers are no longer under the supervision of a child custodian or the discipline of the law but are adult children "by faith in Christ Jesus." It would make no sense for the Galatian believers to give up their superior position of adult sonship in Christ and put themselves under the law.

Second, believers have been baptized by the Spirit into the body of Christ: "For as many of you as have been baptized into Christ have put on Christ" (v. 27). Baptism of the Holy Spirit may be defined as the act of God whereby He places believers into union with Christ and His body, the church, at the moment of salvation (cp. Rom. 6:3-4; 1 Cor. 12:13). The phrase *put on Christ* means to be *clothed* with Him. Dr. Donald Campbell captured the thought well when he wrote, "In the Roman society when a youth came of age he was given a special toga which admitted him to the full rights of the family and state and indicated he was a grown-up son. So the Galatian believers had laid aside the old garments of the Law and had put on Christ's robe of righteousness which grants full acceptance before God. Who would want to don again the old clothing" of the Law?[6]

Third, in Christ believers have the same standing positionally, for "There is neither Jew nor Greek...bond nor free...male nor female; for ye are all one in Christ Jesus" (v. 28). The Lord does not view one believer as superior to another with respect to nationality, status, gender, or social standing. Naturally, this does not do away with a person's physical identity or position in society, but for Christians these distinctions have no meaning because to God Christians are "one" in the body of Christ.

Fourth, all believers, no matter what their distinctions, are the spiritual seed of Abraham: "And if ye be Christ's, then are ye Abraham's seed, and heirs according to the promise" (v. 29). There are four kinds of seed referred to in the Bible: natural, nonspiritual seed (unsaved Jews); natural, spiritual seed (saved Jews); unnatural, nonspiritual seed (unsaved Gentiles); and unnatural, spiritual seed (saved Gentiles). Scripture never teaches that Christians are "spiritual Jews" or "spiritual Israel," as some people teach.

In summary, although the law was holy, just, and good, it did not abrogate the promise of God given in the Abrahamic Covenant, which was ultimately fulfilled in Christ. The law functioned as a mirror to show people that they were unholy, guilty sinners who could not be saved by keeping the law. It functioned as a disciplinarian to reveal the holiness of God and restrict Israel for its own good until Christ (the Son of promise) came to free those who would become children of God the Father (heirs of the promise) through faith in Him. It functioned as a prison, locking people up to faith in Christ as the only means of salvation. But now, everyone who puts his or her faith in Christ for salvation has been set free from the law.

Philip P. Bliss, the great gospel songwriter of the 1800s, caught the meaning of our freedom after meditating on Hebrews 10:10. He then penned the words to "Once for All." The first stanza and the chorus go like this:

> Free from the law, O happy condition!
> Jesus hath bled, and there is remission;
> Cursed by the law and bruised by the fall,
> Grace hath redeemed us once for all.

> Once for all, O sinner, receive it,
> Once for all, O brother, believe it;
> Cling to the cross, the burden will fall,
> Christ hath redeemed us once for all!

Need we say more?

ENDNOTES

[1] Warren W. Wiersbe, *The Bible Exposition Commentary*, Vol. I, Galatians (Wheaton: Victor Books, 1989), p. 701.

[2] Kenneth S. Wuest, *Wuest's Word Studies*, Galatians (Grand Rapids: Wm. B. Edrdmans Publishing Co., 1944), p. 100.

[3] C. Fred Dickason, Jr., *From Bondage to Freedom*, Studies in Galatians, Part 1 (Chicago: Moody Bible Institute, 1963), p. 28.

[4] Wuest, *op. cit.*, p. 107.

[5] Richard N. Longenecker, *Word Biblical Commentary*, Galatians (Dallas: Word Books, 1990), p. 149.

[6] Donald K. Campbell, *The Bible Knowledge Commentary*, Galatians (Wheaton: Victor Books, 1983), Vol. II, p. 600.

Now I say that the heir, as long as he is a child, differeth nothing from a servant, though he be lord of all, But is under tutors and governors until the time appointed of the father. Even so we, when we were children, were in bondage under the elements of the world. But, when the fullness of the time was come, God sent forth his Son, made of a woman, made under the law, To redeem them that were under the law, that we might receive the adoption of sons. And because ye are sons, God hath sent forth the Spirit of his Son into your hearts, crying, Abba, Father. Wherefore, thou art no more a servant, but a son; and if a son, then an heir of God through Christ. Nevertheless then, when ye knew not God, ye did service unto them which by nature are no gods. But now, after ye have known God, or rather are known by God, how turn ye again to the weak and beggarly elements, unto which ye desire again to be in bondage? Ye observe days, and months, and times, and years. I am afraid of you, lest I have bestowed upon you labor in vain. Brethren, I beseech you, be as I am; for I am as ye are; ye have not injured me at all. Ye know how through infirmity of the flesh I preached the gospel unto you at the first. And my trial, which was in my flesh, ye despised not, nor rejected, but received me as an angel of God, even as Christ Jesus. Where is, then, the blessedness ye spoke of? For I bear you witness that, if it had been possible, ye would have plucked out your own eyes, and have given them to me. Am I, therefore, become your enemy, because I tell you the truth? They zealously seek you, but not for good; yea, they would exclude you, that ye might seek them. But it is good to be zealously sought always in a good thing, and not only when I am present with you (Galatians 4:1-18).

7

SONSHIP HAS ITS PRIVILEGES

"...thou art no more a servant, but a son; and if a son, then an heir of God through Christ" (4:7).

The slogan "Membership has its privileges" was popularized by a major American corporation a few years back. The meaning is self-evident: Members of the group are accorded privileges not extended to others.

So it was for those in the Galatian church. They were privileged to be set free from the law's curse, condemnation, and control. They were privileged to be positioned as adult children in God's family forever. They were privileged to be heirs of God according to promise. Yes, the redeemed members of the Galatian church certainly were privileged, yet many were on the brink of setting aside their privileged position in Christ to practice law-keeping, as promoted by the Judaizers.

In Galatians 4:1-18, Paul pressed the analogy of sonship, proving to the Galatians that they should not follow the Judaizers' folly. Doing so would only result in pain and peril for themselves and others.

Possessing Freedom from Legalism

Paul's illustration of sonship was taken from first-century life and showed the inferior position of people living under the Mosaic Law. For example, an "heir, as long as he is a child, differeth nothing from a servant, though he be lord [owner] of all" (v. 1). He had no more rights in his father's house than a slave. He was assigned a tutor (v. 2) who educated and trained him and, in general, watched over him. He was also assigned a governor who functioned as a manager or steward of his estate until he reached the legal age to access his inheritance. Such was the case "until the time appointed of the father" (v. 2). Then a ceremony was held recognizing that the son had reached adulthood and was entitled to enjoy all the rights of his position. For the Jewish lad, the ceremony is called a *bar mitzvah* and is held on his 13th birthday. The Roman father determined the age at which his son was formally considered to be an adult, whereupon he received the *toga virilis*. The Greek child was under his father's control until the age of 18, whereupon an elaborate ceremony was held acknowledging his coming of age.

Like a child, said Paul, "we...were in bondage under the elements of the world" (v. 3). All children are immature and under the "elements," or basic principles put forth by their religions in this world system. For the Jews, it was the system of symbols, ceremonies, and legal enactments that Judaism required. For the Gentiles, it was the ceremonies and rituals practiced in their pagan religions.[1] Thus, the apostle concluded that all people were enslaved, like children, to their religious systems until Christ came to liberate them spiritually.

No adult in his or her right mind would return to the bondage of a second childhood. But that is exactly what the Galatian believers would be doing if they embraced the Judaizers' position. Therefore, "Legalism...is not a step toward maturity, it is a step back in childhood."[2]

With the words, "But...God" (v. 4), Paul abruptly broke into his argument to show that God did not leave people living under the law without hope; for "when the fullness of the time was come, God sent forth his Son" (v. 4) to redeem mankind. When the exact historical moment appointed by the Father arrived, Jesus Christ came into the world.

The world had been prepared for the Messiah's birth in a number of marvelous ways. Religiously, Israel had put away its idolatry, Old Testament revelation was complete, synagogues had been planted throughout the Middle East, and a messianic expectancy existed in all of Judæa. Religiously, the Gentile world was hopelessly controlled by Greek philosophies, pagan mythology, and immoral practices in their worship, which left the people spiritually bankrupt and desperately in need of a Savior. Politically, Rome had established a *Pax Romana* (*Roman Peace*) and built a network of roads throughout the Mediterranean world, making travel to major cities safe. Roman law guaranteed civil rights to the people, and Roman legions stationed throughout the area assured political stability. Socially, the Greek culture and language had united the area, making the proclamation of the gospel easier. It was at this appointed time in history that "God sent forth his Son" (v. 4).

He was sent forth not only as the eternal, divine Son, but as the incarnate Son as well: "made of a woman, made under the law" (v. 4). He was the God-Man—commissioned by God the Father and virgin born—who voluntarily placed Himself under the Mosaic Law, submitting Himself to its restrictions and requirements like any other Judæan of that day.

God sent His Son for two reasons. First, "To redeem them that were under the law" (v. 5). The word *redeem (exagorase)* means to *buy out of the slave market.* The emphasis of redemption is not on the penalty of the law's curse, mentioned earlier (3:13), but on the bondage (slavery) of the entire Mosaic system.[3] Thus, it made no sense for the Galatian believers to once again place themselves under the law's bondage. In so doing, they would be saying to the world that Christ's redemptive death on the cross was meaningless and unnecessary.

Second, Christ redeemed people from the law's slavery so "that we might receive the adoption of sons" (v. 5). No longer are believers minors under the law, but mature children set free, bought out of slavery, and brought into the Father's house with all the legal rights of sonship. The Greek word *adoption (huiothesia)* means to *place one as an adult son in a family.* Because believers become children of God only through the new birth, we are called adoptive children of the Father. All adoptive children are "heirs of God, and joint heirs with Christ" (Rom. 8:17) and will receive their full inheritance at their change (1 Th. 4:17-18), which is called "the redemption of [the] body" (Rom. 8:23).

God confirmed their adoption as children by sending "the Spirit of his Son into [their] hearts, crying, Abba, Father" (v. 6). *Abba* is an Aramaic word for *father*, equivalent in English to *daddy* or *papa.* It speaks of the intimate trust, confidence, and reliance a child has in his or her father, wherein the child is able to call upon him for any need. The Holy Spirit brings believers into this very intimate relationship with the Father. When interceding in Gethsemane just before His crucifixion, Jesus uttered the words "Abba, Father" (Mk. 14:36), expressing His total trust in God. In like manner, Christians can put the same explicit confidence in God as their Father, trusting Him to sustain them—through the Holy Spirit's ministry—during their darkest hours.[4]

A beautiful contrast between those who are children and those who are mere servants is made by Dr. Warren Wiersbe. First, the child is born into the family, but the servant is not (Lk. 15:18-19). Second, the child possesses the same nature as the father (2 Pet. 1:4), but the servant does not. Third, the child has a father (Rom. 8:15-16), but the servant has a master. Fourth, the child obeys out of love (Rom. 5:5; Jn. 14:15), but the servant obeys out of fear. Fifth, the child is rich (Gal. 4:7), but the servant is poor. Sixth, the child is disciplined under grace, but the servant is disciplined under the law. Seventh, the child has a future, but the servant does not.[5] Who in their right mind would give up such a privileged position in Christ to place themselves under the law's bondage?

Pitfalls of Following Legalism

The apostle went on to remind the Galatians that by embracing legalism they would be returning to bondage—a bondage similar to that which they had experienced as heathens "when [they] knew not God, [and] did service unto them which by nature are no gods" (v. 8), like Zeus and Hermes (Acts 14:11-13).

Perplexed over their desire to keep the law, Paul drew attention to their folly by asking a rhetorical question: "But now, after ye have known God [by experiencing personal salvation, not just in an intellectual sense], or rather are known by God [God recognizing their personal commitment to Christ and showing them favor[6]], how turn ye again to the weak [powerless] and beggarly [bankrupt] elements [principles], unto which ye desire again to be in bondage?" (v. 9). Returning to their former state would be returning to a rudimentary religious system that was bankrupt and powerless to set people free from sin's enslavement.

Paul indicated that the Galatians had already begun to turn toward keeping the Mosaic Law, although they had not yet yielded to circumcision (Gal. 5:1-6). They were observ-

ing "days [sabbaths and feast days], and months [the seventh month or new moons], and times [seasonal feasts], and
years [sabbatical and jubilee years]" (v. 10; cp. Col. 2:16),
hoping to gain spiritual privileges from God. This was the
point of Paul's position: "works could not be added to faith
as ground for either justification or sanctification."[7]

The apostle voiced his deep concern about their departure into Judaism: "I am afraid of you [fear for you], lest I
have bestowed upon you labor in vain" (v. 11).   If the
Galatians returned to legalism, Paul's labor (to the point of
exhaustion) in taking the gospel to them was all for naught
(cp. 1:6; 2:21).

People who keep the Old Testament law, even apart
from the motive of gaining spiritual privileges before God,
are treading on dangerous ground, whether they are Jewish
or Gentile believers.

Many pastors, like the apostle, have preached their
hearts out and spent hours disciplining their congrega-
tions, only to find that some have regressed into unscrip-
tural teachings or legalism or are following fraudulent
fanatical teachers who rob them of the spiritual freedom
provided in Christ.

Plea to Forsake Legalism

With a heart full of love and deep concern for the
Galatians, Paul made a passionate personal appeal, beg-
ging them to "be [become] as I am; for I am as ye are" (v.
12).   He wanted them to become free from the law's
bondage, as he did at his conversion. The apostle had set
aside the Mosaic Law as a way of gaining favor with God
and had become like the Gentiles, who were never under
the law.   Paul assured the Galatians that they had not
offended him, for they had "not injured [him] at all" (v. 12);
it was purely for their spiritual well-being.

The apostle reminded them of the great stress he was

under at their first meeting: "Ye know how through infirmity of the flesh I preached the gospel unto you at the first" (v. 13). He did not reveal what kind of "infirmity" he had. Scholars speculate that Paul's infirmity could have been malaria; disfigurement and weakness due to a beating suffered at Lystra (Acts 14:19); eye trouble, possibly an eye disease known as ophthalmia (a running of the eyes) because he wrote with such large letters (6:11); or a physical problem brought about by his "thorn in the flesh" (2 Cor. 12:7). Whatever the infirmity, it was so repulsive that it caused people to loathe and reject him. The text seems to indicate that he had an eye disease such as ophthalmia.

But the Galatians had neither "despised...nor rejected" (v. 14) him for the "trial, which was in [his] flesh" (v. 14). Rather, they had received him "as an angel of God, even as Christ Jesus" (v. 14). This was most likely a reference to the time when Paul healed the lame man at Lystra (Acts 14:6-13).

The Galatians had been so blessed by the apostle's ministry that they "would have plucked out [their] own eyes" (v. 15) to replace Paul's afflicted eyes. They would have made any sacrifice for the apostle because of their love for him.

Bewildered over the Galatians' attitude and actions, the apostle asked, "Where is, then, the blessedness ye spoke of?...Am I, therefore, become your enemy, because I tell you the truth?" (vv. 15-16). That is, Have you lost your joy? Do you now look upon me as your enemy because I honestly confronted you with the truth about your departure into legalism? (How many pastors face the same attitude when confronting people about erring from the truth?)

Paul's motive toward the Galatians was genuine. He was like a loving father protecting his children from wrong. But the Judaizers' motive was not as genuine. They were "zealously" courting the Galatians, "but not for good" (v. 17). Their plan was to "exclude [shut off]" (v. 17) the Galatians from Paul's fellowship so that they would only have the Judaizers to "seek" (v. 17) for spiritual fellowship and guidance.

The apostle agreed that "it is good to be zealously sought," if it is for good (v. 18). He had courted the Galatians with honorable motives, having their spiritual interest in mind, whether present with them or absent from them. He was not against other spiritual leaders courting them, if they had good intentions and it was for their spiritual well-being. But he opposed the Judaizers adamantly because they were corrupting the church with their fallacious teachings.

Believers must stand against modern-day Judaizers who unscrupulously twist the gospel with their legalistic teachings. They are wolves in sheep's clothing, passing themselves off as angels of light, going about like roaring lions, or creeping into Christian fellowships, seeking to bring believers into bondage.

Remember, privileged children of God, we are members of Christ's body, adopted as adult children into His family, set free from the curse, condemnation, and control of the law. Therefore, stand fast in liberty. Do not succumb to legalism.

ENDNOTES

[1] Kenneth S. Wuest, *Wuest's Word Studies*, Galatians (Grand Rapids: Wm. B. Eerdmans Publishing Co., 1944), p. 114.

[2] Warren W. Wiersbe, *The Bible Exposition Commentary*, Galatians (Wheaton: Victor Books, 1989), Vol. I, p. 706.

[3] Donald K. Campbell, *The Bible Commentary*, Galatians (Wheaton: Victor Books, 1983), Vol. II, p. 601.

[4] Lehman Strauss, *Devotional Studies in Galatians and Ephesians* (Neptune: Loizeaux Brothers, Inc., 1957), p. 57.

[5] Wiersbe, *op. cit.*, pp. 706-707.

[6] Campbell, *op. cit.*, p. 602.

[7] Wuest, *op. cit.*, p. 124.

My little children, of whom I travail in birth again until Christ be formed in you, I desire to be present with you now, and to change my tone; for I stand in doubt of you. Tell me, ye that desire to be under the law, do ye not hear the law? For it is written that Abraham had two sons, the one by a bondmaid, the other by a freewoman. But he who was of the bondwoman was born after the flesh; but he of the freewoman was by promise; Which things are an allegory; for these are the two covenants: the one from the Mount Sinai, bearing children for bondage, who is Hagar. For this Hagar is Mount Sinai in Arabia, and answereth to Jerusalem which now is, and is in bondage with her children. But Jerusalem which is above is free, which is the mother of us all. For it is written, Rejoice, thou barren that bearest not; break forth and cry, thou that travailest not; for the desolate hath many more children than she who hath an husband. Now we, brethren, as Isaac was, are the children of promise. But as then he that was born after the flesh persecuted him that was born after the Spirit, even so it is now. Nevertheless, what saith the scripture? Cast out the bondwoman and her son; for the son of the bondwoman shall not be heir with the son of the freewoman. So then, brethren, we are not children of the bondwoman, but of the free (Galatians 4:19-31).

8

TWO TYPES OF SONS

"...brethren, we are not children of the bondwoman,
but of the free" (4:31).

The joys of giving birth are great, but so can be the
agony of guiding that child to maturity. What is
true in the physical realm is also true in the spiritual realm.
Paul rejoiced over the spiritual birth of the Galatians, but,
like a mother in great travail for a wayward child, he strug-
gled to guard his children from the corrupt teachings of the
Judaizers.

Before concluding his defense, the apostle gave one
final warning to the Galatians—a warning couched in a
pointed analogy between Hagar and Sarah and their two
sons, Ishmael and Isaac. The warning beautifully illus-
trates the differences between the legalistic bondage being
promoted by the Judaizers and the freedom the Galatians
enjoyed in Christ. But first Paul took off the hat of a stern

theologian and put on the hat of a loving pastor as he corrected his spiritual children.

Paul's Compassion

With deep affection the apostle wrote, "My little children, of whom I travail in birth again until Christ be formed in you" (v. 19). The phrase *little children*, used only this one time in Galatians, means *dear born ones* and expressed Paul's deep concern for their welfare. He had travailed in giving new birth to them, but once again he travailed over their well-being. The Galatians were making the maternal heart of Paul undergo birth pains a second time. This was abnormal and unnatural, making him feel like a mother who had to deliver the same baby twice.[1]

But Paul was willing to suffer along with the Galatians "until Christ be formed in" them. The word *formed* means *transformed* or a *metamorphosis* of Christ-likeness taking place in their spiritual lives. He desired that Christ be completely formed in the believers (Gal. 2:20), making them immune to the Judaizers' false doctrine.

For some reason Paul was unable to visit the Galatians, but he wanted to be with them to "change [his] tone" (v. 20). It is always better to deal with a problem face to face rather than from a distance, for then people can put more *heart* into their voices, something that is impossible to do in a letter.

Because the Galatian believers leaned toward the Judaizers' position, Paul stood "in doubt [perplexed] of" them (v. 20). He was at his wit's end, puzzled at how to once and for all convince them to leave the error of legalism.[2]

Portrait of Comparisons

It has often been said, "A picture is worth a thousand words." To indelibly etch his point on the Galatians' minds, Paul drew upon a well-known incident from the

Old Testament as a fitting illustration and conclusion to the matter of law and grace, hoping that this would forever wean them away from the Judaizers' error.

The illustration centered on Abraham's two sons and their mothers, which Paul called "an allegory" (v. 24). An allegory can be defined as "a narrative or word picture—an extended metaphor, either true to life or fictitious, with many parts pointing symbolically to spiritual realities, designed to teach spiritual truths by comparison."[3] Thus, the passage can be read on either a literal or symbolic level. By calling this section an allegory, Paul was in no way doubting the literal interpretation of the Genesis account or its historical trustworthiness. The words "Which things are an allegory" (v. 24) are better translated "which sort of things are being set forth in allegory."[4] Paul's allegory was an illustration or analogy in which he pointed out that certain facts about Hagar corresponded to non-believers, while certain facts about Sarah corresponded to believers.[5]

It is important to understand the difference between an allegory and allegorizing. Allegorizing is taking license with Scripture where the interpreter seeks a deeper meaning in the text, often called "spiritualizing." Paul was not doing this.

Paul's allegory accomplished seven objectives in his fight against the Judaizers' heretical position. First, it focused on both Abraham and the law (Judaizers supported both) to prove that justification is by faith. Second, the apostle proved his position by using the Judaizers' own style of rabbinical exegesis and argument. Third, it illustrated and reviewed all the major points of his position and, in so doing, proved that the principles found in the law led to bondage, whereas a life of faith leads to freedom. Fourth, the account in Genesis is a very emotional story, providing a fitting conclusion to his argument. Fifth, it pointedly told the Galatians that they should cast out the legalizers. Sixth, the allegory pulled together all of the doctrinal principles and practical applications Paul had been making. Seventh, it led right into the next chapter, in which the apostle began the practical section of his letter.[6]

The Galatians had not yet adopted the law, but they were near the point of doing so. Appealing to their intelligence, Paul said, "Tell me, ye that desire to be under the law, do ye not hear the law?" (v. 21). That is, Do you really know what you are about to embrace? Do you really know what the law says? Most likely you do not because you have not studied its principles or given heed to all of its laws and commands.

The Judaizers prided themselves in being the physical seed of Abraham and partakers of the Mosaic Law. Paul used their background to make four comparisons of the differences between law and grace, once and for all negating their legalistic position.

He began by comparing the conceptions of Ishmael and Isaac (Gen. 16; 17; 21), Abraham's two sons. First he dealt with the mothers who conceived them. Ishmael, Abraham's first son, was borne by Hagar, "a bondmaid," and Isaac was borne by Sarah, "a freewoman" (v. 22) who was Abraham's wife. Hagar was a slave; thus, her son Ishmael was also a slave. Because Sarah was a freewoman, her son Isaac was also free. Surely the Galatians would understand the analogy. By embracing the law, they portrayed themselves as sons born in bondage, thereby disqualifying themselves as heirs of the covenant promises.

Next, Paul dealt with the manner of the sons' conceptions. Ishmael was naturally conceived by Hagar, "the bondwoman...after the flesh," but Isaac was conceived by Sarah, "the freewoman...by promise" (v. 23). Isaac was born both naturally and through supernatural (miraculous) intervention because Abraham and Sarah were past the age of childbearing (Gen. 18:11; Rom. 4:18-21). This meant that Ishmael by birth had no share in the inheritance of the covenant promises of Abraham, but Isaac, the true heir by birth, had a right to the covenant promises. "Wherefore she said unto Abraham, Cast out this bondwoman and her son; for the son of this bondwoman shall not be heir with my son, even with Isaac. And the thing was very grievous in Abraham's sight because of his son. And God said unto Abraham, Let it not be grievous in thy sight because of the lad, and because of thy bondwoman; in all that Sarah hath said unto thee, hearken unto her voice; for in Isaac shall thy seed be called" (Gen. 21:10-12). In like manner, the Judaizers were trying to give legitimacy to their position of adding law to grace as the only means by which eternal life could be inherited. But, as Paul argued, this was impossible, for the law brought about bondage and could never impart spiritual life (Gal. 3:21), righteousness (Gal. 2:21), the gift of the Spirit (Gal. 3:2), or spiritual inheritance (Gal. 3:18).[7]

Paul's second comparison was of the two covenants. The Mosaic Covenant was made at "Mount Sinai, bearing children for bondage, who is Hagar" (v. 24). Although not stated, the other covenant, made with Abraham, was a covenant of grace and promise representing Sarah. Hagar produced children born into slavery, as did the Mosaic Covenant, which was based on the law. Sarah produced children of freedom through the Abrahamic Covenant, which was based on promise. Dr. Warren Wiersbe wrote, "Whosoever chooses Hagar (Law) for his mother is going to experience bondage (Gal. 4:8-11, 22-25, 30-31; 5:1). But whoever chooses Sarah (Grace) for his mother is going to enjoy liberty in Christ. God wants His children to be free."[8]

Paul's third comparison was to two cities. "Hagar is Mount Sinai in Arabia, and answereth to Jerusalem which now is, and is in bondage with her children. But Jerusalem which is above is free, which is the mother of us all" (vv. 25-26).[9] Hagar stood for the Mosaic Covenant ratified at Mount Sinai. Her son Ishmael stood for Jerusalem, which was in bondage to the Romans, stripped of freedom, and under the Mosaic Law. Sarah represented (although not stated; cp. Heb. 12:18-24) the New Covenant ratified by Christ's blood on the cross. Her son Isaac stood for the heavenly Jerusalem, which is free from the law, slavery, fleshly works, and unrighteousness and is the dwelling place of God and departed saints.

The two sons had the same father but different mothers. Although they had a similar heritage and environment, they were completely different in nature. Paul's point was that it is not enough to claim the same father; both Jews and Christians can do that. But to which mother were you born? Those born to Hagar are in bondage and have no part in the inheritance of the heavenly Jerusalem. Those born to Sarah are children of freedom and heirs of the promised inheritance, the heavenly Jerusalem.

Paul's fourth comparison was of the two types of children coming from the two women. Quoting from the Septuagint version of Isaiah 54:1, he wrote, "Rejoice, thou barren that bearest not; break forth and cry, thou that travailest not; for the desolate hath many more children than she who hath an husband" (v. 27). Originally, Isaiah's prophecy referred to Israel before, during, and after the Babylonian Captivity. But in this context Paul applied the verse to Sarah and Hagar's spiritual offspring. Sarah, who was originally barren, eventually gave birth to a son, and in time her descendants outnumbered those of Hagar. The point of Paul's analogy was that God has supernaturally intervened to give spiritual birth to the church, made up of both Jews and Gentiles who will greatly outnumber those living in bondage under the Mosaic Law.

Practical Conclusion

Paul concluded his argument by presenting three personal applications. First, he compared the children: "Now we, brethren, as Isaac was, are the children of promise" (v.

28). Isaac, born of Sarah, the freewoman, was a son of promise who was supernaturally conceived. In the same manner, all believers are supernaturally conceived through the new birth (Jn. 3:3, 5) and are spiritual seed of Abraham and heirs according to promise (3:7-9, 18, 29). Paul was speaking of the time when believers will stand before God. Their fate will not rest upon their spiritual descendants or law-keeping but upon the unconditional aspect of the promises given to Abraham by grace.[10]

Second, he mentioned a spiritual conflict being waged: "as then he that was born after the flesh persecuted him that was born after the Spirit, even so it is now" (v. 29). Paul was referring to Ishmael's persecution of Isaac (cp. Gen. 21:8-9). He paralleled this persecution with the conflict he and the Galatian believers were suffering at the hands of the Judaizers. The Judaizers (a type of Ishmael) were born out of legalistic self-effort and were persecuting Paul and all true believers (a type of Isaac) who were born by grace through faith.[11]

Third, in contrast to the attitude of the persecutors was the command from God, "Cast out the bondwoman and her son; for the son of the bondwoman shall not be heir with the son of the freewoman" (v. 30). Although these words were originally uttered by Sarah, God confirmed that Abraham should follow Sarah's desire (Gen. 21:9-10, 12). It was self-evident that the two sons and their mothers could not dwell in the same household, for the older, Ishmael (about 17 years old), would mock and corrupt Isaac, the true heir of the Abrahamic promises. The separation was to be permanent: "Cast out the bondwoman." It is not possible to mix or reconcile law and grace or faith and works. Legalism, as a way to gain favor with God or a rule of life, must be once and for all expelled and excluded from the lives of believers.

Paul brought his argument to a climactic conclusion

with the words, "So then, brethren, we are not children of the bondwoman, but of the free" (v. 31). All true believers have been liberated by Christ; they are to stand in this liberty and never embellish it with legalism.

The apostle provided a choice for the Galatians that applies to us today. Do we want to be children of Ishmael, who was conceived after the flesh, whose mother was a slave, who lived in the bondage of an earthly Jerusalem, and who was under a covenant of legalism? Or do we want to be children of Isaac, who was conceived through supernatural intervention, whose mother was free, who was positioned in the heavenly Jerusalem, and who was under the New Covenant of grace? The choice is yours! Whose child are you?

ENDNOTES

[1] John MacArthur, *The MacArthur New Testament Commentary*, Galatians (Chicago: Moody Press, 1987), p. 120.

[2] *Ibid.*, p. 122

[3] Roy B. Zuck, *Basic Bible Interpretation* (Wheaton: Victor Books, 1991), p. 221.

[4] C. Fred Dickason, Jr., *From Bondage to Freedom, Studies in Galatians* (Chicago: Moody Bible Institute, 1963), Part II, p. 6.

[5] *Op. cit.*, Zuck, p. 47.

[6] James Montgomery Boice, *The Expositor's Bible Commentary*, Galatians (Grand Rapids: Zondervan Publishing House, 1976), Vol. X, p. 482.

[7] Warren W. Wiersbe, *The Bible Exposition Commentary*, Galatians (Wheaton: Victor Books, 1989), Vol. I, p. 713.

[8] *Ibid.*, p. 713.

[9] Lehman Strauss, *Devotional Studies in Galatians and Ephesians*, (Neptune: Loizeaux Brothers, Inc., 1957), p. 69.

[10] *Op. cit.*, Dickason, p. 9.

[11] Donald K. Campbell, *The Bible Knowledge Commentary*, Galatians (Wheaton: Victor Books, 1983), Vol. II, p. 604.

Stand fast, therefore, in the liberty with which Christ hath made us free, and be not entangled again with the yoke of bondage. Behold, I, Paul, say unto you, that if ye be circumcised, Christ shall profit you nothing. For I testify again to every man that is circumcised, that he is a debtor to do the whole law. Christ is become of no effect unto you, whosoever of you are justified by the law; ye are fallen from grace. For we through the Spirit wait for the hope of righteousness by faith. For in Jesus Christ neither circumcision availeth anything, nor uncircumcision, but faith which worketh by love. Ye did run well; who did hinder you that ye should not obey the truth? This persuasion cometh not of him that calleth you. A little leaven leaveneth the whole lump. I have confidence in you through the Lord, that ye will be none otherwise minded; but he that troubleth you shall bear his judgment, whosoever he be. And I, brethren, if I yet preach circumcision, why do I yet suffer persecution? Then is the offense of the cross ceased. I would they were even cut off who trouble you (Galatians 5:1-12).

9

LIVING IN LIBERTY

"Stand fast...in the liberty with which
Christ hath made us free..." (5:1).

Patrick Henry wrote, "Is life so dear or peace so sweet as to be purchased at the price of chains and slavery? Forbid it, almighty God! I know not what course others may take, but as for me, give me liberty or give me death." Swayed by the impassioned words of this great patriot, the Revolutionary Convention was moved to arm the American colonies for their coming struggle against the British.

In like manner, Paul dealt with a liberty-or-death issue facing the Galatian church, which needed to arm itself against the Judaizers' deadly doctrine of circumcision. The Judaizers taught that circumcision was necessary for salvation, but if this doctrine was embraced, it would strip the church of its freedom in Christ and put it in the death grip of legalistic bondage.

Knowing that the Judaizers would try to sway the Galatians to their position, Paul armed the new believers with a biblical defense, a quick-hitting arsenal of practical exhortations designed to destroy the shackles of legalism and prove that believers should continue to stand in the liberty provided through Christ.

Command to Stand in Liberty

Paul began by commanding the Galatians to "Stand fast [keep on standing], therefore, in the liberty [freedom] with which Christ hath made us free" (v. 1). This was the theme of the apostle's letter and the end result of justification by faith. This command functions as a summary of the doctrinal section of the epistle (Gal. 3-4) and an introduction to the practical section (Gal. 5:1-6:10).

Not only were the Galatian believers to stand in liberty, they were to shun legalism: "and be not [stop being] entangled again with the yoke of bondage" (v. 1). Legalism has a twofold effect on people who are caught in its web. First, they are like animals or birds ensnared in a trap, the trap of legalistic Judaism—a system of religious dos and don'ts. Second, they are under "the yoke of bondage," a picture of servitude. Peter used the term *yoke* at the Jerusalem Council when he referred to yoking Gentile believers to the law, which neither past generations of Jewish people nor the apostles were able to bear. Peter said, "Now, therefore, why put God to the test, to put a yoke upon the neck of the disciples, which neither our fathers nor we were able to bear?" (Acts 15:10).

Although Christians are to throw off the yoke of legalism, they must put themselves under Christ's yoke, which is described as "easy" and "light" (Mt. 11:29-30). Dr. Warren Wiersbe has well said, "The unsaved person wears a yoke of sin (Lam. 1:14); the religious legalist wears a yoke of bondage (Gal. 5:1); but the Christian who depends on God's grace wears the liberating yoke of Christ."[1]

Consequences of Succumbing to Legalism

Paul used the issue of circumcision to illustrate his point concerning liberty. The Judaizers taught the Galatians that they had to be circumcised to be saved, but the apostle reminded them, "if ye be circumcised, Christ shall profit you nothing" (v. 2).

Paul was not condemning the practice of circumcision, for he had Timothy (whose mother was Jewish) circumcised in Galatia so that he could have a ministry among his people (Acts 16:1-3). He was not saying that Galatian believers who were circumcised had lost their salvation, for Jesus clearly stated that those who are given eternal life "shall never perish, neither shall any man pluck them out of my hand...[nor] out of my Father's hand" (Jn. 10:28-29). He was not saying that the Galatians had already turned to the Judaizers' practice of circumcision. The words *if ye be* indicate a hypothetical situation. Paul was saying that if the Galatian believers allowed themselves to be circumcised, they would promote a false teaching that would have no spiritual benefit for their salvation. The Jerusalem Council also had to deal with this problem.

Paul warned the Galatian believers of four consequences they would experience if they succumbed to the legalists' demands. First, if they were circumcised, Christ would profit them nothing (v. 2). Those who believed that circumcision was necessary for salvation, spiritual growth, and advancement or that it bestowed added grace to their spiritual lives would be adding works to saving faith. By doing so, the believers would be supplementing Christ's work with human works, thereby making Christ of no profit to themselves (cp. 2:19-20; 3:3, 12; 4:3, 9; 5:7, 18).

Second, any believer who embraced the law by practicing circumcision would be "a debtor [obligated or bound] to do the whole law" (v. 3). God presented the Mosaic Law as a unified system, and those living under the Mosaic system were legally obligated to keep all of its commandments. Failure to do so put people under its curse (cp. 3:10; Jas. 2:10). People could not simply pick and choose the laws they wanted to keep; they had to keep the *whole* Mosaic system if they chose to put themselves under it. But, as Paul taught earlier in this epistle, Christians must die to the law to gain life in Christ (2:19-20).

Third, "Christ is become of no effect" for those who were trying to be "justified by the law" (v. 4). Paul was not speaking about their position in salvation but about their present spiritual experience in Christ. The apostle often referred to the Galatians as *brethren* and used the personal pronoun *we* (linking them to himself as fellow believers) throughout this epistle. Furthermore, the words *become of no effect (katergeo)* mean *to render inoperative*. When Christians put themselves under the law to be justified or sanctified, they are making Christ inoperative in their spiritual walk, which can result in a fall from grace (v. 4) or being cut off from the blessings and fellowship of the indwelling Holy Spirit needed to live fruitful lives in Christ.

Fourth, embracing the law would result in being cut off from "the hope of righteousness [which is] by faith" (v. 5). Again, Paul was not referring to salvation but to the completed righteousness that believers will experience at their glorification (Rom. 8:29-30). At the moment of salvation, believers receive the imputed righteousness of Christ by faith. But it is the completed "hope of righteousness" that believers are eagerly awaiting. They hope for the day when the Lord will come to rapture them away, resulting in their glorification, the consummation of their salvation (Rom. 8:30; 1 Cor. 15:51-52). Those living under the law had no assurance that God would declare them righteous. Only those who by faith receive Christ possess this personal assurance—an assurance that is confirmed by the indwelling Holy Spirit (Rom. 8:16).

In concluding his illustration on circumcision, Paul said, "For in Jesus Christ neither circumcision availeth anything, nor uncircumcision, but faith which worketh by love" (v. 6). Circumcision plays no role in salvation, nor does it please God. God is pleased by faith working through the love principle, because love is a fulfillment of the law (v. 14). People who live by faith are energized through love, not by some external, legalistic system. Therefore, people who put themselves under a bankrupt legalistic system cut themselves off from the life of liberty and fellowship that Christ has lovingly provided.

Confronting the Saints over Legalism

Paul abruptly concluded his argument on circumcision and confronted the Galatians about their readiness to embrace legalism by comparing their Christian experience to a race—one of the apostle's favorite metaphors. "Ye did run well [conducted yourselves honorably]; who did hinder you [cut you off] that ye should not obey the truth?" (v. 7; cp. Rom. 9:16; 1 Cor. 9:24-26; Gal. 2:2; 2 Tim. 4:7). The Galatians had run the Christian race superbly in the past, but someone had thrown them off stride, causing them to stumble, slowing down their progress toward the goal. The word *who* refers to the Judaizers, who were trying to compete and complete the race through legalism and self-effort rather than by faith. The apostle assured them that "This persuasion [the Judaizers' seductive words] cometh not of him [God] that calleth you" (v. 8). God never calls people to salvation through self-effort but by the gospel through faith (Eph. 2:8-9).

Paul compared these false teachers and their doctrine to leaven: "A little leaven leaventh the whole lump" (v. 9). Leaven is often used in the Bible as a symbol of evil or corruption. Jesus warned His disciples to be on guard against the "leaven [false teachings] of the Pharisees and of the

Sadducees" (Mt. 16:6, 12). Paul referred to immorality within the church as leaven (1 Cor. 5:6). False doctrine, if not dealt with, will spread within a church, causing its complete corruption. The point of Paul's analogy is clear. Just as a little leaven placed in dough soon spreads throughout the entire batch, so the Judaizers' false teaching, if allowed to exist, would permeate the entire Galatian church. Like leaven, doctrinal heresy works its way through a church slowly, often unnoticed, until it has corrupted the whole congregation. False teaching cannot be controlled, reasoned with, or dealt with slowly but must be quickly removed.

Although the Galatians were leaning toward the Judaizers' position, Paul said, "I have confidence in you through the Lord, that ye will be none otherwise minded" (v. 10). Paul had a settled confidence in his heart that the Galatians would not turn from the truth of the gospel to embrace the false doctrine being propagated by the Judaizers. In fact, he wanted the one responsible for troubling or disturbing the Galatians to "bear his judgment, whosoever he be" (v. 10). He wanted to see the full weight of God's grievous judgment fall on any of the Judaizers who attempted to lead these babes in Christ into the destructive doctrine of legalism (cp. Mt. 18:6; 2 Pet. 2:9). Paul was probably referring to the future day of God's judgment as well as to present-day church discipline.

Countering the Seductive Legalists

Unable to counter Paul's argument, the Judaizers attacked the apostle, accusing him of preaching circumcision whenever it suited his purpose. They charged that he preached the necessity of circumcision to Jews but not to Gentiles. True, Paul had preached circumcision before his conversion. True, he had Timothy circumcised because he was from a Jewish background (Acts 16:1-3). True, he did not compel Titus (a Gentile) to be circumcised (Gal. 2:3).

But he never promoted the practice as being necessary for salvation. In fact, Paul refuted such accusations, first because he was being persecuted by Judaism: "And I, brethren, if I yet preach circumcision, why do I yet suffer persecution?" (v. 11). The fact that Paul suffered persecution at the hands of Judaism disproved the Judaizers' accusation. Second, if Paul was still preaching the need for circumcision, "Then is the offense of the cross ceased" (v. 11) or become inoperative. The cross was an offense or stumbling block to the Jews (Rom. 9:33; 1 Cor. 1:23) because it provided freedom from the Mosaic Law through Christ's death. If Paul had preached circumcision (which he did not), then the cross no longer would have been an offense to the Jews.

Paul concluded this section of his letter with a sarcastic comment to discredit the Judaizers: "I would they were even cut off [mutilated] who trouble you" (v. 12). Paul wished that the Judaizers who were troubling the Galatians would go beyond circumcision and completely emasculate (castrate) themselves, as some heathen priests did. (This is a reference to Cybele, a Phrygian goddess, whose priests and many of her followers castrated themselves.) Paul was implying that if, like the pagans, the Galatians believed that legalism could earn them divine favor, they should go to the pagan extreme of self-mutilation. But such an act would, according to the Mosaic Law, disqualify them from God's service. Paul made the point that circumcision (law-keeping) could not contribute to a person's justification or sanctification.

Oswald Chambers provides a fitting conclusion to Paul's exhortation: "Always keep your life measured by the standards of Jesus. Bow your neck to His yoke alone, and to no other yoke whatever; and be careful to see that you never bind a yoke on others that is not placed by Jesus Christ...There is only one liberty, the liberty of Jesus at work in our conscience enabling us to do what is right."[2]

May we, like Paul, cast off the chains of legalism and choose to stand in Christ's liberty.

ENDNOTES

[1] Warren W. Wiersbe, *The Bible Exposition Commentary*, Galatians (Wheaton: Victor Books, 1989), Vol. I, p. 713.

[2] Oswald Chambers, *My Utmost For His Highest* (New York: Dodd, Mead & Company, 1935), p. 127.

For, brethren, ye have been called unto liberty; only use not liberty for an occasion to the flesh, but by love serve one another. For all the law is fulfilled in one word, even in this: Thou shalt love thy neighbor as thyself. But if ye bite and devour one another, take heed that ye be not consumed one of another. This I say then, Walk in the Spirit, and ye shall not fulfill the lust of the flesh. For the flesh lusteth against the Spirit, and the Spirit against the flesh; and these are contrary the one to the other, so that ye cannot do the things that ye would. But if ye be led by the Spirit, ye are not under the law. Now the works of the flesh are manifest, which are these: adultery, fornication, uncleanness, lasciviousness, Idolatry, sorcery, hatred, strife, jealousy, wrath, factions, seditions, heresies, Envyings, murders, drunkenness, revelings, and the like; of which I tell you before, as I have also told you in time past, that they who do such things shall not inherit the kingdom of God. But the fruit of the Spirit is love, joy, peace, long-suffering, gentleness, goodness, faith, Meekness, self-control; against such there is no law. And they that are Christ's have crucified the flesh with the affections and lusts. If we live in the Spirit, let us also walk in the Spirit. Let us not be desirous of vainglory, provoking one another, envying one another (Galatians 5:13-26).

10

VICTORIOUS CHRISTIAN LIVING

**"If we live in the Spirit, let us also
walk in the Spirit" (5:25).**

"How should we then live?" asked Dr. Francis A.
Shaeffer in his best-selling book by that title. His
question centered on how Christians should live in the
midst of a declining Western culture in which lust, license,
and liberation from authority were gaining worldwide
acceptance.

The Galatian believers faced the same issue in their day.
How were they to live out their new liberty in Christ?
Should they embrace the legalistic principles taught by the
Judaizers? Should they follow others who were manifest-
ing libertine tendencies?

Paul anticipated the question. In his final polemic
denouncing legalism and defending the doctrine of

Christian liberty, the apostle focused his attention on this very important issue. In Galatians 5:13 to 26 Paul defined true Christian liberty and instructed believers how to lead victorious Christian lives.

Christian Freedom Controlled

Paul reminded the Galatian believers that they had been "called unto liberty" but quickly charged them not to use their "liberty for an occasion to the flesh" (v. 13). The apostle was not referring to the physical body but to the sin nature with its lustful appetites that long for self-gratification. He exhorted Christians to guard against giving their old sin nature an "occasion" (starting point of operation) to manifest evil.

Christian commitment carries with it an ethical command to love and serve others (v. 13). Believers are to voluntarily show a self-sacrificing, *agape*-type love and serve others with the attitude of bond slaves. Building on this thought, Paul went on to remind the Galatians that the "law [the whole Mosaic system] is fulfilled in one word...Thou shalt love thy neighbor as thyself" (v. 14). Believers who love at all times will not violate the rights of others, will voluntarily look out for their neighbors' welfare, and will seek to minister to their brothers and sisters in Christ (cp. Mt. 22:36-40). Believers must be filled with love that is produced by the Holy Spirit to have the power and desire to manifest this kind of service.

If liberty in Christ is not controlled by love, conflict is sure to arise. Apparently this took place within the Galatian church. They were beginning to "bite and devour one another" (v. 15). People who practice legalism within the church often cause strife and schism rather than spiritual unity. On the other hand, people who express their Christian liberty often fail to manifest it in love and wisdom, thereby disrupting church unity. Thus, liberty or the lack of it must be under the control of the Holy Spirit if unity is to be maintained.

Christian Fleshly Conflicts

A spiritual war is raging within Christians between their sin nature and their spiritual nature. How can we gain victory over the sin nature? Judaizers would argue that Christians need the restraining influence of the law to hold their sin nature in check. Paul argued just the opposite. He said that the key is to "Walk in the Spirit, and ye shall not fulfill the lust of the flesh" (v. 16). The solution to overcoming the old nature is not through law-keeping or self-effort but by the indwelling power of the Holy Spirit, who enables believers to live holy lives (Rom. 7:7-8:4). Herein lies the secret to spiritual victory in our lives. Christians who yield to the Holy Spirit's control moment by moment will not succumb to temptation and gratify the sins of their flesh.

Paul further described the battle between the two natures when he wrote, "For the flesh lusteth against the Spirit, and the Spirit against the flesh; and these are contrary the one to the other, so that ye cannot do the things that ye would" (v. 17). Each nature has strong desires, the Adamic nature pulling toward committing sin and the new nature toward holy living (cp. Rom. 7:7-25). Thus, believers "cannot do the things that [they] would" (v. 17). The sin nature blocks believers from doing good, while the Holy Spirit blocks them from doing evil in this ongoing warfare.

Believers are not passive in the battle. They are free to choose which nature they will serve. "But," said Paul, "if ye be led by the Spirit, ye are not under the law" (v. 18). That is, those who are led by the Holy Spirit are provided the freedom and power in their new nature to live above legalism or license.

The Apostle then listed "the works of the flesh" (v. 19), dividing them into four categories.

Sexual Sins (v. 19)

1. "Adultery" and "fornication" (KJV) or *porneia* (original Greek)—*immorality* in general and equivalent to the English word *pornography*, referring to illicit sex. Such sexual acts as adultery, fornication, incest, homosexuality, prostitution, and bestiality are in this category.

2. "Uncleanness" *(akatharsia)*—impurity in thoughts and actions.

3. "Lasciviousness" *(aselegia)*—a debauched lifestyle that indulges in brazen expression of base sexual desires without restraint, shame, or concern for others. The current free expression of sex and pornography and the spread of sexually transmitted diseases are good examples of lasciviousness.

Spiritual Sins (v. 20)

1. "Idolatry"—worship of man-made idols.

2. "Sorcery," from which the word *pharmacy* comes—speaks of the use of drugs in witchcraft and black magic, practices that are prevalent today.

Social Sins (vv. 20-21)

1. "Hatred"—a feeling of enmity and hostility, especially within groups.

2. "Strife"—contention, quarreling, and fighting, which are the natural results of hatred and are often expressed within Christian groups.

3. "Jealousy"—a sin that is against others.

4. "Wrath"—unrestrained outbursts of violent anger, the result of seething anger.

5. "Factions"—strife resulting from a self-seeking, self-serving, selfish attitude.

6. "Seditions"—discord and dissension causing

divisions among people.

7. "Heresies"—factions formed by those who chose to depart from the fundamental doctrines of the Christian faith, subverting it and causing schisms in the church, such as the Judaizers.

8. "Envyings"—the evil desire to take and possess what belongs to another.

9. "Murders"—the premeditated taking of human life.

Surfeiting Sins (v. 21)

"Drunkenness" and "revelings"—occur when a rowdy, boisterous, intoxicated person carouses at night and becomes involved in orgies that are connected to pagan worship. Paul added the words "and the like" to indicate that he had not presented an exhaustive list of "the works of the flesh."

The apostle included the sober warning that those "who do such things [i.e., habitually practice these sins] shall not inherit the kingdom of God" (v. 21). He was not saying that Christians can lose their salvation by committing any of the sins mentioned but that the habitual practice of such sins would indicate that the people committing them are not saved.

How, then, are believers to deal with their sin nature so that they will not commit the sins of the flesh? Paul gave the answer: "they that are Christ's have crucified the flesh with the affections [disposition to sin] and lusts [desires]" (v. 24). Paul was not referring to mutilation of the body or self-crucifixion to overcome the desires of the flesh. Nor did he indicate that the sin nature has been eradicated or rendered inactive in Christians. He had already shown that those who come to Christ have been crucified with Him (2:20). When sinners are converted, their identification with Christ's death on the cross results in the power of the old sin nature to be broken in their lives. Thus, believers have potential victory over sin by the indwelling Holy Spirit, which provides them with the needed power to shun the affections and lusts of their flesh when tempted to do evil.

Christian Fruitful Conduct

The Spirit not only provides believers with the power to live victoriously over the old sin nature but will produce fruit in the lives of yielded believers (Jn. 15:1-5). Fruit is always the outward manifestation of the inner life. Note that the word *fruit* is singular. It is "the *fruit* of the Spirit" (v. 22) not "*fruits* of the Spirit," as some state.

The apostle listed nine Christian virtues produced by the Holy Spirit through the new nature in believers controlled by Him. They are divided into three categories.

Psychological Christian Virtues (v. 22)

1. "Love"—*agape* love, a self-sacrificing love that is the foundation of all Christian virtues produced by Spirit-controlled believers. Paul provides a beautiful description of agape love in 1 Corinthians 13.

2. "Joy"—a deep-seated, inner happiness or well-being that only God can produce and that is not dependent on outward circumstances, either favorable or unfavorable, in our lives (cp. Jn. 15:11).

3. "Peace"—that inner tranquillity of soul and spirit in the midst of adversity that is given by the Lord (Jn. 14:27) and transcends human understanding (Phil. 4:7). This type of peace is manifested in harmonious relationships with fellow Christians and to those with whom believers come in contact through their daily walk (1 Th. 5:13).

Public Christian Virtues (v. 22)

1. "Long-suffering"—willingness to patiently endure wrong and ill-treatment without retaliation.

2. "Gentleness"—treating others with the same concern and kindness that God manifests to believers.

3. "Goodness"—manifesting moral uprightness and good will to those who are undeserving (Lk. 10:30-35).

Personal Christian Virtues (vv. 22-23)

1. "Faith" (lit., faithfulness)—not the expression of personal faith but faithfulness and trustworthiness in ordering our walk before the Lord.

2. "Meekness"—not weakness but a humble attitude of spirit toward God and gentle consideration of others in the midst of correcting their attitudes or actions.

3. "Self-control"—personal rule or mastery over the spirit, desires, or fleshly impulses that would be impossible without the Holy Spirit's control.

Paul brought his argument to a close by stating, "against such there is no law" (v. 23). God does not make laws against these things, nor would mankind make laws prohibiting the practice of such virtues. These are the very virtues that God desires believers to manifest in their Christian walk. Those who are living out these concepts need no laws to keep them in check or produce righteous attitudes and actions.

Believers, having been united with Christ through His crucifixion and resurrection, are to walk according to the enabling power of the Holy Spirit: "If [because] we live in the Spirit, let us also walk in the Spirit" (v. 25). The word *walk* in verse 16 means to *walk about or order our manner of life in a way that glorifies God.* In verse 25, the word for *walk* is a military term that means to *go step by step in a straight line, always guiding to the right when marching in rank and file with the one leading.* What a beautiful picture of Christians ordering their conduct under the guidance and power of the Holy Spirit.

The apostle concluded this section of his epistle with a warning to two groups of Galatian believers: "Let us not be desirous of vainglory, provoking one another, envying one another" (v. 26). The first group was not to use its liberty for license, seeking "vainglory," an attitude of conceit or pride that lifts self above other Christians in their freedom. Such people tend to flaunt their liberty before weaker believers who are more legalistic and bound by conscience not to express their faith with the same liberty. The second group was composed of weaker believers who were to guard against envying and judging the former group (cp. 1 Cor. 6:7-13).

Such self-seeking attitudes from either group would be a manifestation of the flesh and would produce provocation and envy within the church. It is a stench in the nostrils of God. Believers are to walk free of the sins of pride and envy.

How should Christians then live? In a balanced Christian walk totally controlled by the Holy Spirit. Doing so requires two simple steps. First, realize and rely on the fact that you have been crucified with Christ at the moment of salvation. Therefore, the power of sin no longer has control over your life. Second, yield moment by moment to the indwelling Holy Spirit's filling and control. The results will be life-changing, to say the least.

Although the temptation to commit sin will naturally arise, you will possess the needed power to live victoriously over such lusts of the flesh. Although others may walk in conflict with fellow Christians, your heart will be full of love, and you will serve your neighbor, whom you will love as yourself. Although others may be filled with pride, seeking vainglory and provoking fellow believers to envy, humility will be your portion. Finally, if you practice these principles, you cannot help but manifest the fruit of the Spirit.

Herein lies the secret to victorious Christian living.

Brethren, if a man be overtaken in a fault, ye who are spiritual restore such an one in the spirit of meekness, considering thyself, lest thou also be tempted. Bear ye one another's burdens, and so fulfill the law of Christ. For if a man think himself to be something, when he is nothing, he deceiveth himself. But let every man prove his own work, and then shall he have rejoicing in himself alone, and not in another. For every man shall bear his own burden. Let him that is taught in the word share with him that teacheth in all good things. Be not deceived, God is not mocked, for whatever a man soweth, that shall he also reap. For he that soweth to his flesh shall of the flesh reap corruption; but he that soweth to the Spirit shall of the Spirit reap life everlasting. And let us not be weary in well doing; for in due season we shall reap, if we faint not. As we have, therefore, opportunity, let us do good unto all men, especially unto them who are of the household of faith (Galatians 6:1-10).

11

SPIRIT-LED SERVICE

"As we have...opportunity, let us do good
unto all men, especially unto them
who are of the household of faith" (6:10).

"Though every believer has the Holy Spirit, the Holy Spirit does not have every believer," wrote A. W. Tozer. Many Christians find it easy to talk about being Spirit-filled but show little evidence of it in their daily walk.

Being Spirit-filled is not some mystical experience or so-called "second work of grace." Nor does some ecstatic utterance of an unknown tongue signify that the person speaking has been Spirit-filled. Being Spirit-filled involves continual, moment-by-moment control by the Holy Spirit in the lives of believers. Those filled with the Spirit will manifest the fruit of the Spirit (Gal. 5:22-23) in their character and service. In Galatians 6:1-10 Paul gave a series of practical examples on how Spirit-led believers are to live.

Sinners Restored

Spirit-led believers are in touch with the needs of their brothers. The apostle illustrated this through a hypothetical example of a brother caught in sin. "Brethren, if a man be overtaken in a fault, ye who are spiritual restore such an one" (v. 1). The word *fault* has the idea of *slipping* or *lapsing* into sin. Some interpret the word *overtaken* to mean that he was caught in the act of sinning. Others teach that believers carelessly living in the flesh can be overtaken by sin before they are aware of committing the offense. This interpretation fits the context

In cases like these, a person who is "spiritual" (Spirit-filled) should help restore sinning believers back to fellowship. The word *restore* was used in the first century to describe setting a broken or dislocated bone. It was also used to describe fishermen mending their nets. Setting bones and mending nets must be done with great care and precision. Spiritual people are to carry out their ministry of restoration in a "spirit of meekness"—with gentleness and love (v. 1). The emphasis is not on the brother's sin but on his restoration.

How would legalists try to restore a sinning brother? Legalists are often in competition with their brothers, displaying an air of self-righteousness; therefore, they most likely would condemn the brother rather than show compassion or concern (cp. Lk. 18:9-14).

Paul cautioned those involved in restoration, "[consider] thyself, lest thou also be tempted" (v. 1). *Consider* means to *look at the matter with continual diligence*, guarding against falling into the same appeal to commit sin. Restorers must guard against self-righteous attitudes by looking down on the ones to whom they are ministering. They must remember that they are subject to like temptations and, in a weak moment, could themselves fall. Peter is a good illustration of this. He promised not to deny the Lord (Mt. 26:33), but within a matter of hours he denied Him three times (Mt. 26:34, 69-75).

The same weaknesses are seen in Christian workers today. In recent years numerous leaders have succumbed to sins that they had condemned from the pulpit. Paul has well stated, "let him that thinketh he standeth take heed lest he fall" (1 Cor. 10:12).

People seeking to restore a brother have the responsibility of bearing his burden. "Bear ye one another's burdens, and so fulfill the law of Christ" (v. 2). The *burden* is any weight or load too heavy to bear. The word is used figuratively and refers to any temptation, sin, or moral weakness too difficult for a brother to overcome. In this context, it could have been pressure from the Judaizers to embrace their legalistic position. Others in the fellowship are to bear their brother's burden as if it is their own. They are to give sympathy, comfort, counsel, and a helping hand when needed.

Christians who take on this commitment "fulfill [satisfy the requirements of] the law of Christ [the law given by Christ]" (v. 2). The commandment to "love one another" (Jn. 13:34; 15:12; Gal. 5:13-14; 1 Jn. 3:23) fulfills all other laws because it "worketh no ill" to anyone else or to society in general (Rom. 13:8, 10).

Legalists practice just the opposite. They impose heavy commitments on their followers but never lift a finger to ease the load (Mt. 23:4). On the other hand, Christ bears the burdens of all believers (1 Pet. 5:7) and desires that His children do likewise.

Christians talk and sing about love and bearing one another's burdens, but all too often they do not become involved. Excuses are myriad: "I don't have the time." "I have my own problems." "I'm not experienced." Even some pastors guard their time so closely that they thrust some of their responsibilities on others within the church.

Self-Reflection

In seeking to be burden bearers, Christians must guard against an attitude of spiritual superiority toward sinners. Paul said, "if a man think himself to be something, when he is nothing, he deceiveth himself" (v. 3). People who think they are spiritually superior in such situations are self-deceived and commit the sin of spiritual pride. The best of people, held up to the standards of a Holy God, are nothing: "For I know that in me (that is, in my flesh) dwelleth no good thing" (Rom. 7:18). Christians have no reason to lift themselves above a brother because everything they are and have was provided by God (1 Cor. 4:7). People with this type of attitude are not Spirit-led. Those who are spiritually proud are disqualified from helping others because they have distorted vision. They must first remove the log that is in their own eye before they can see to remove the speck from their brother's eye (Mt. 7:1-5).

It is crucial, therefore, that Christians examine themselves to "prove [their] own work" (v. 4). *Prove* means *to put to the test* for approval. Believers should compare their walk to God's standard, not to their brother's; then they can "have rejoicing in [themselves] alone, and not in another" (v. 4). There is no thought of overestimating self or excessive boasting in this passage. Rather, it speaks of proper rejoicing as an approved servant before God.

People who test their own works find that they too have burdens to bear. Paul reminded us that "every man shall bear his own burden" (v. 5). There may seem to be a contradiction between verses 2 and 5, but this is not the case. The word for *burden (baros)* in verse 2 refers to a heavy, oppressive load, the weight of which is too great for a person to carry alone. Conversely, the word for *burden (portion)* in verse 5 refers to a lightweight pack that can be carried on the back. Believers have a responsibility to bear personal burdens that are light and bearable. All Christians are responsible for their own conduct and service, for which they will give an account at the Bema judgment (1 Cor. 3:10-15; 2 Cor. 5:10). Such knowledge should preclude any feeling of spiritual superiority or spiritual comparison among believers.

Sharing Resources

Paul provided his readers with a practical way for believers in Christ to communicate (*koinoneo*) [v. 6] with one another. The word *communicate* means *to participate in a common fellowship of sharing*. It is difficult to know exactly what the apostle meant by "share...in all good things" (v. 6). Some scholars believe he was referring to financial support in return for spiritual help. Elsewhere he instructed that "the elders that rule well be counted worthy of double honor [financial remuneration], especially they who labor in the word and doctrine" (1 Tim. 5:17; cp. 1 Cor. 9:7-14). Others believe he meant to provide mutual encouragement within the fellowship and was not referring to financial gifts to those who minister.

Many scholars embrace the latter position for several reasons. First, the context speaks of evil (vv. 1-5) and moral good (vv. 9-10), not financial support. Second, the *good things* in context are defined as spiritual, not material. Third, Paul would not have admonished the Galatians to support their teachers for fear that the Judaizers would be quick to accuse him of attempting to win over the Galatians for his own financial gain. Fourth, Paul's enemies were always quick to say that he was in the ministry for financial gain. Fifth, Paul was seeking to encourage the Galatian believers to continue fellowshipping with the grace teachers around the Word of God for mutual enrichment and to forsake following the Judaizers.

Sowing and Reaping

Paul issued a strong warning to those Galatian believers who did not think it mattered which group of teachers they followed (teachers of grace or Judaizers). He commanded, "Be not deceived [lit., stop being deceived]" (v. 7). If they did not think it mattered which teachers they followed, they were already self-deceived. This type of attitude mocks God (v. 7). Mocking is *turning up the nose at, ignoring,* or *holding in contempt.* But God cannot be "mocked" by mankind (v. 7). He is unaffected by anything we think or do. Therefore, people holding this attitude are hurting only themselves.

God is never inconsistent in applying His divine law of sowing and reaping. That which is true in the physical realm of sowing and reaping is also true in the spiritual realm: "whatever a man soweth, that shall he also reap" (v. 7). This law is immutable: "he that soweth to his flesh shall of the flesh reap corruption; but he that soweth to the Spirit shall of the Spirit reap life everlasting" (v. 8).

The word *flesh* refers to the old nature that manifests the sins already mentioned (5:19-21). The result is corruption—a picture of spoiled crops decaying in the field, which no farmer would reap. If eaten, spoiled crops can cause severe sickness or even death. In the spiritual realm, sowing to the flesh ultimately leads to destruction and death (Jas. 1:13-15). Those following the Judaizers' pseudoreligious system of works/righteousness were sowing to the flesh. Embracing this position produced a harvest of spiritual degeneration and decay and eventually spiritual death.

What about Christians who sow to the flesh? Will they be separated from Christ? No, but they will lose the joy of their salvation, experience an unfruitful spiritual life, and be subject to chastisement.

Those who sow "to the Spirit," said Paul, "reap life everlasting" (v. 8). They will receive eternal life along with a harvest of spiritual blessings in this life and into eternity.

The apostle gave a promise to encourage any of the Galatian believers who were becoming discouraged by the continual grind of fighting the Judaizers or receiving little appreciation for living a good life in Christ. He wrote, "And let us not be weary in well doing; for in due season we shall reap, if we faint not" (v. 9).

Sowing in the Lord's service is often hard and can be extremely tiring. Some do not see immediate results from their efforts and become weary and faint while serving. But those who persevere in well doing will reap in due season. A Spirit-filled walk keeps believers from losing heart, relaxing in their service, and giving up before the harvest.

Crops are reaped at various times in nature, and the same is true of spiritual reaping. Some reaping will be realized in this life, but only the judgment seat of Christ will reveal the full harvest that believers will reap. In light of this, Christians must guard against becoming lax in their daily living for the Lord or shrinking back in their service for Him. Those who faint forfeit future rewards.

Spiritual Responsibility

Knowing that they will reap what they sow, believers have a spiritual responsibility to "do good unto all men, especially unto them who are of the household of faith" (v. 10). With these words, Paul pulled together his primary teaching in Galatians 5:13-6:10. Only Spirit-filled believers can show this kind of love to other people.

Jesus said that it is impossible to say we love the world of ungodly people if we do not love our fellow Christians (Jn. 13:34-35; 1 Jn. 3:14; 4:20-21). When is this love to be shown? "As we have, therefore, opportunity, let us do good" (v. 10). The word *opportunity* means a *seasonable or appropriate time*. The exhortation is not just to do good when some special opportunity arises or when we feel like it, but to look for occasions in this season of life while we have the opportunity. Right now we are to sow "good" (that is, *spiritual benefits and blessings)* to everyone, whether spiritual or material.

To carry out Paul's instructions concerning burden bearing and sowing good to those around us, we must be filled with the Holy Spirit. Dr. Elwood Stakes, founder of the famous Ocean Grove Religious Community in New Jersey, was moved by the same need. In 1879 he wrote the song, "Hover O'er Me, Holy Spirit." John R. Sweney, camp meeting musical director, wrote the music. "While on my knees in prayer, God seemed to speak the melody right into my heart," said Sweney. The third stanza of this simple gospel hymn speaks to our need: "I am weakness, full of weakness. At Thy sacred feet I bow; Blest, divine, eternal Spirit, Fill with pow'r, and fill me now. Fill me now, fill me now, Jesus, come and fill me now; Fill me with Thy hallowed presence, Come, O come, and fill me now."

We must continually ask ourselves the question posed by Dr. Tozer: "Though we have the Holy Spirit, does the Holy Spirit have us?"

Ye see how large a letter I have written unto you with mine own hand. As many as desire to make a fair show in the flesh, they constrain you to be circumcised; only lest they should suffer persecution for the cross of Christ. For neither they themselves who are circumcised keep the law, but desire to have you circumcised, that they may glory in your flesh. But God forbid that I should glory, except in the cross of our Lord Jesus Christ, by whom the world is crucified unto me, and I unto the world. For in Christ Jesus neither circumcision availeth anything, nor uncircumcision, but a new creature. And as many as walk according to this rule, peace be on them, and mercy, and upon the Israel of God. Henceforth let no man trouble me; for I bear in my body the marks of the Lord Jesus. Brethren, the grace of our Lord Jesus Christ be with your spirit. Amen (Galatians 6:11-18).

12

THE FINAL WARNING

**"...God forbid that I should glory, except in
the cross of our Lord Jesus Christ..." (6:14).**

Vance Havner once said, "Contending for the faith is
not easy. It is not pleasant business. It has many
perils. It is a thankless job, and it is highly unpopular in an
age of moral fogs and spiritual twilights. It is nicer to be an
appeaser than an opposer."

The Apostle Paul was no appeaser. He was not trying
to win any popularity contests. He was a soldier of the
cross who opposed those who tried to subvert the doctrine
of salvation by grace through faith, apart from any work of
the law. He fought hard against people who tried to under-
mine Christian freedom in Christ. To those who doubted
his true motive Paul could show the scars of sincerity—
scars resulting from stoning, scourging, self-denial, and
other struggles he faced defending the truth of the gospel.

In the closing verses of the Epistle to the Galatians, Paul personalized the abstract principles he had argued throughout his letter by comparing his motive with those of the Judaizers.

Paul's Writing

The apostle often dictated his letters to an *amanuensis* (*one employed to write from dictation or to copy manuscripts*), but he wrote the salutations and conclusions in his own hand, proving that the letter was genuine. He made sure that the Galatians realized that he was the author of this letter by stating, "Ye see how large a letter I have written unto you with mine own hand" (v. 11). Some scholars interpret the words "how large a letter" to mean that Paul wrote in large letters because of bad eyesight (cp. 4:13-15). Others say he wrote in Greek *uncials* (*large block letters*) rather than the cursive style of a scribe. Still others believe that the apostle was referring to writing his conclusion in capital letters (the Greek text says "letters" not "letter") to emphasize the importance of his teachings throughout the epistle. The correct interpretation is debatable, but Paul's motive is certain. In these latter verses he again reminded his readers of the letter's authenticity and reviewed its major themes.

Paul's Warning

Paul warned the Galatians of the Judaizers' motive. They were not interested in the Galatians' spiritual well-being but wanted "to make a fair show in the flesh"; thus they "constrain you to be circumcised" (v. 12). They were interested only in making converts to their position and parading them before others to receive the praise of men. Often the true motive of churches or individuals who boast of the many people they have won to the Lord, baptized, or had join the church is dubious. It may not be to praise the Lord but to win the praise of men.

One reason the Judaizers practiced circumcision was to

avoid "suffer[ing] persecution for the cross of Christ" (v. 12). They identified with the church but not with the cross. They were not ready to embrace the shame of the cross suffered by the followers of the one who had died on it, under the curse of the law. By embracing circumcision they hoped to sidestep the wrath of the Jewish leaders, who were severely persecuting the Christians while at the same time trying to win them to their own position.

The cross stood for rejection and shame in that day. It was the most inhumane, dehumanizing death possible. Its purpose was to humiliate and prolong the suffering of the one being crucified. The condemned person hung naked for everyone to see and suffered excruciating physical and mental pain, sometimes for days, before succumbing to death. Such punishment was ordered by Roman law against enemies of the state or those committing serious crimes against society. Because crucifixion was a severe form of capital punishment, Roman citizens were exempt from it.

One author has beautifully stated, "Yet this symbol of a horrible means of death became for Christians the most cherished symbol of life, because Christ had suffered and died on a cross as the full and final sacrifice to save them from sin and death. God transformed the most fearful expression of man's hatred into the most beautiful expression of His divine love. Paul presented the cross often in this epistle (2:20; 3:1; 5:11, 24; 6:12, 14) because through it God provided His redemptive grace to mankind."[1]

To the Jewish people the preaching of the cross was "a stumbling block" and to the Gentiles it was "foolishness," but to Christians "it is the power of God" unto salvation (1 Cor. 1:18-25). Jesus made it very clear: "If any man will come after me, let him deny himself, and take up his cross, and follow me" (Mt. 16:24); "And he that taketh not his cross and followeth after me, is not worthy of me" (Mt. 10:38).

Paul accused the Judaizers of hypocrisy. They masked

their true motives by demanding that Gentiles be circumcised and keep the Mosaic Law, but they did not practice what they preached: "For neither they themselves who are circumcised keep the law" (v. 13).

They were like the scribes and Pharisees whom Jesus mentioned in Matthew 23, who demanded that their followers practice religious rituals that they themselves did not keep. Jesus called such people "fools" (v. 17), "hypocrites" (vv. 23, 25, 27, 29), "serpents," and a "generation of vipers" (v. 33). Like the Pharisees, the Judaizers were practicing things through which they could "glory in [the] flesh" (v. 13).

Christians must guard against the same attitudes and practices. It is possible to be actively involved in the Lord's work for the wrong motives—spiritual pride or self-praise.

Paul's Walk

In contrast to the Judaizers, who gloried in human achievement, Paul "glor[ied]...in the cross of...Christ" (v. 14). He knew well of what he spoke, for in the past Paul had been a Pharisee, a religious zealot whose zeal for the law was unparalleled in Judaism. After coming to Christ, however, he counted it all as loss compared to the excellency of knowing Christ Jesus (Phil. 3:4-9). With a strong negative—"God forbid" (perish the thought) [v. 14]—he showed extreme disgust for glorying in anything other than the cross of Christ. But the apostle could glory in the cross, which is a symbol of the entire system of salvation and Christian belief.

Paul gave three reasons why he gloried in the cross. The first was his commitment: "the world is crucified unto me, and I unto the world" (v. 14b). The word *world* denotes everything that is outside of and opposed to the things of Christ. It refers to the spiritual and moral character of this age of grace. Since the fall of Adam and Eve, all ages have been in spiritual darkness, greatly affected by Satan, "the prince of the power of the air" (Eph. 2:2). Believers have been freed from this evil system through the cross of Christ. Paul said that he was dead to the world's evil system; it had no control over him. His motives were Christ-centered, not world-centered. He wanted the Galatians to follow him and his doctrine, not the fleshly doctrine of the Judaizers.

Paul's second reason for glorying in the cross was that believers are set free from the ceremonial law: "For in Christ Jesus neither circumcision availeth anything, nor uncircumcision, but a new creature [creation]" (v. 15). Practices such as circumcision for the Jews or uncircumcision for the Gentiles do not provide a means of salvation (cp. 5:6). Salvation and a radical change in character are obtainable only through the work of Christ on the cross. No one can become a new creature by keeping ceremonial laws.

Paul's third reason for glorying in the cross was that it is the only way through which believers can order their conduct in a way that pleases the Lord: "And as many as walk [order their conduct] according to this rule, peace be on them, and mercy, and upon the Israel of God" (v. 16). His point was that the Galatians (especially the Judaizers among them) could choose how they would order their conduct regarding their acceptance of the grace of Christ through faith. The word *rule (kanon)* means *a principle or standard of measurement.* Believers are to order their conduct by the principles and standards of the gospel through the indwelling Holy Spirit, who empowers them to do so (cp. 5:16-17, 25). In so doing, they experience the "peace...and mercy" of God (v. 16). Conversely, those who refuse to walk according to this rule do not experience God's peace and mercy.

Some scholars believe that Paul's reference to "the Israel of God" (v. 16) applies to all true believers—Jews and Gentiles—who make up the church. This cannot be the correct interpretation for a number of reasons. First, the phrase "and upon the Israel of God" is an afterthought to the general benediction and shows Paul's desire for Jewish people who embrace the gospel of Christ to receive God's peace and mercy, referring to the true remnant within Israel (cp. Rom. 9:6, 27; 11:5). In this passage Paul recognized the true Jewish believers within the church.[2] Second, the word *and* can be translated *even* (NIV), identifying "the Israel of God" as Jewish believers within the church. Third, the other 65 uses of the term *Israel* in the New Testament refer to the Jewish people. It would be strange for Paul to refer to Gentile Christians as "Israel." Fourth, Paul elsewhere referred to two kinds of Israelites—believers and unbelievers (Rom. 9:6).[3] It is clear that the phrase "the Israel of God" refers only to Jewish believers within the church.

Paul's Wounds

Having fully dealt with the Judaizers' legalism, Paul had one final word to the Galatian church on the subject: "Henceforth let no man trouble me; for I bear in my body the marks of the Lord Jesus" (v. 17). He was not implying that he did not want to hear about problems or troubles the Galatian believers were facing. Nor was he asking the Judaizers to stop causing trouble for him. Rather, he was asking the Galatians to stop causing trouble for him by following the heretical practices and teachings of the Judaizers, for he bore in his body scars caused by his stand for the truth of the gospel of Christ as a committed servant of the Lord.

The word *marks (Gr., stigmata)* means *brand* and was often used in Paul's day to denote ownership. Before his conversion Paul bore the mark of circumcision to identify himself as a Jew, but now he bore the marks of Christ, which identified him as a Jewish believer. The word was used in many different ways. Slaves in the Phrygian temples were branded with the name of their deity, showing that they were committed to serve that god for life.

Likewise, Paul bore in his body the marks of service to his God (Col. 1:24). Soldiers were often marked with the name of their commanding general, indicating complete allegiance to him. Paul endured hardship as a good soldier of Christ; he kept the faith, fought a good fight, and finished the course laid out for him (2 Tim. 2:3; 4:7). Slaves were marked with a brand bearing the name of their owners. At the beginning of his epistles, Paul often identified himself as a servant (bond slave) of Christ (Rom. 1:1).[4] Criminals were marked with a brand to identify them in society. Paul was branded as a criminal for the sake of the gospel and bore the marks of scourging, chains, and months spent in prison (2 Cor. 11:23-24). One writer states, "Paul's body, marked by the assaults made upon his person, must often have been wracked with pain. Paul was a man old before his time, partly by reason of the sufferings..."[5] (cp. 2 Cor. 4:8-11; 6:4-10; 7:5; 12:7-10).

In closing his letter, Paul showed deep affection for the Galatians, calling them "Brethren" (v. 18). Ending as he began, he pronounced a benediction on his readers: "the grace of our Lord Jesus Christ be with your spirit" (v. 18; cp. 1:3). One writer aptly called this "A final declaration of grace over law."[6] Paul ended his letter with "Amen" (so be it) [v. 18], affirming all that he had said between the two *graces*.

George Bennard went through a very difficult experience that caused him to reflect on the significance of the cross and what the Apostle Paul meant when he spoke of entering into the fellowship of Christ's sufferings. While contemplating Paul's experience, Bennard was convinced that the cross was not just a religious symbol but the heart of the gospel. In 1913, while ministering in Albion, Michigan, he wrote the beloved hymn, "The Old Rugged Cross." The last two stanzas go like this:

In the old rugged cross,
   stained with blood so divine,
      A wondrous beauty I see;
For 'twas on that old cross
   Jesus suffered and died
      To pardon and sanctify me.

To the old rugged cross
   I will ever be true,
      Its shame and reproach gladly bear;
Then He'll call me some day
   To my home far away,
      Where His glory forever I'll share.[7]

Friend, will you, like Paul, bear the shame and reproach of the Christ who died on the old rugged cross, thus proclaiming that salvation comes by grace through faith—plus nothing?

ENDNOTES

[1] John MacArthur, *The MacArthur New Testament Commentary*, Galatians (Chicago: Moody Press, 1987), p. 199.

[2] C. Fred Dickason, Jr., *From Bondage to Freedom, Studies in Galatians* (Chicago: Moody Bible Institute, 1963), Part II, p. 28.

[3] Donald K. Campbell, *The Bible Knowledge Commentary*, Galatians (Wheaton: Victor Books, 1983), Vol. II, p. 611.

[4] Kenneth Wuest, *Wuest's Word Studies*, Galatians (Grand Rapids: Wm. B. Eerdmans Publishing Co., 1944), p. 179.

[5] *Ibid.*, p. 180.

[6] MacArthur, *op. cit.*, p. 211.

[7] Kenneth W. Osbeck, *101 Hymn Stories* (Grand Rapids: Kregel Publications, 1979), p. 255.

RECOMMENDED READING

Boice, James Montgomery, *The Expositor's Bible Commentary*, Galatians (Grand Rapids: Zondervan Publishing House, 1976).

Campbell, Donald K., *The Bible Knowledge Commentary*, Galatians (Wheaton: Victor Books, 1983).

DeHaan, M. R., *Galatians* (Grand Rapids: Radio Bible Class, 1960).

Dickason, Jr., C. Fred, *From Bondage to Freedom: Studies in Galatians* (Chicago: Moody Bible Institute, 1963).

Gromacki, Robert G., *Galatians: Stand Fast in Liberty* (Grand Rapids: Baker Book House, 1968).

Ironside, H. A., *Expository Messages on the Epistle to the Galatians* (Neptune, NJ: Loizeaux Brothers, 1940).

Longenecker, Richard N., *Word Biblical Commentary*, Galatians (Dallas: Word Books, 1990).

Luther, Martin, *Commentary on Galatians* (Grand Rapids: Kregel Publications, reprint of 1525).

MacArthur, John Jr., *The MacArthur New Testament Commentary*, Galatians (Chicago: Moody Press, 1987).

MacDonald, William, *Believer's Bible Commentary*, Galatians (Nashville: Nelson Publishers, 1990).

McGee, J. Vernon, *Thru the Bible with J. Vernon McGee*, Galatians (Neptune, NJ: Loizeaux Brothers, 1957).

Tenney, Merrill C., *Galatians: The Charter of Christian Liberty* (Grand Rapids: Wm. B. Eerdmans Publishing Co., 1954).

Wiersbe, Warren W., *The Bible Exposition Commentary*, Galatians (Wheaton: Scripture Press Publications, Victor Books, Vol. 1, 1989).

Wuest, Kenneth S., *Wuest's Word Studies*, Galatians (Grand Rapids: Wm. B. Eerdmans Publishing Co., Vol. 1, 1944).

PART II
JUDE

INTRODUCTION

Jude called himself "the servant of Jesus Christ, and brother of James" (v. 1). The name *Jude* is derived from *Judah* and pronounced *Judas* in Greek. It was a very common name in the first century. Five men named *Judas* are mentioned in the New Testament: Judas, an apostle who was "the son of James" (Lk. 6:16; Acts 1:13); "Judas Iscariot, who also was the traitor" (Lk. 6:16); Judas, the brother of James and half brother of Jesus (Mt. 13:55); Judas of Damascus (Acts 9:11); and "Judas, surnamed Barsabbas" (Acts 15:22). Neither of the two apostles named Judas can be the author of this book because Jude never called himself an apostle. Judas of Damascus and Judas Barsabbas are eliminated because they did not have a brother named James. That leaves only Judas the brother of James and half brother of Jesus to have written the Book of Jude.

Jude did not record the date of his writing, but he referred to 2 Peter 3:3 in Jude 18, which gives some indication of when he penned the epistle. Scholars date Peter's writing around 65-66 A.D., and Jude wrote soon after that, possibly around 67-68 A.D. Although the location where the book was written is not given, many believe it to have been Jerusalem.

Jude had started to write about the "common salvation" (v. 3) provided in Christ, but the Holy Spirit directed him to warn the church about false teachers (possibly Gnostics) who were coming into the fellowship with their ungodly teachings (v. 4). Jude begged the church to stand against such individuals and "earnestly contend for the faith which was once delivered unto the saints" (v. 3).

Most likely Jude wrote to Hebrew Christians because many of his references were from the Old Testament. But the letter was circulated to all the churches warning them of ungodly teachers.

Jude wrote in figurative language, drawing many illustrations from nature and from individuals who were apostates in the Old Testament. He built figure upon figure, often writing in triads—sanctified, preserved, called (v. 1); mercy, peace, love (v. 2)—to make his point. The theme of the Book of Jude is "earnestly contending for the faith." The key words are "remember" and "ungodly"; the key verses are 3 and 4.

OUTLINE

I. PRESERVED FROM APOSTASY (vv. 1-2)
   A. Servant of Christ (v. 1)
   B. Selected in Christ (v. 1)
   C. Sanctified by Christ (v. 1)
   D. Secure in Christ (v. 1)
   E. Sustained by Christ (v. 2)

II. PROBLEM OF APOSTASY (vv. 3-4)
   A. Common Faith (v. 3)
   B. Contending for the Faith (v. 4)
   C. Corruption of the Faith (v. 4)
   D. Conduct of the False Teachers (v. 4)

III. PAST APOSTATES (vv. 5-7)
   A. Failure of Israel (v. 5)
   B. Fall of Angels (v. 6)
   C. Fornication of Sodom and Gomorrah (v. 7)

IV. PRESENT APOSTATES (vv. 8-11)
   A. Defiled Dreamers (v. 8)
   B. Disputing the Devil (v. 9)
   C. Destruction Declared (v. 10)
   D. Destiny Described (v. 11)

V. PROFILE OF APOSTATES (vv. 12-16)
   A. Character of Apostates (vv. 12-13)
      1. Worthless Worship (v. 12)
      2. Wicked Shepherds (v. 12)
      3. Waterless Clouds (v. 12)
      4. Withered Trees (v. 12)
      5. Wind-tossed Waves (v. 13)
      6. Wandering Stars (v. 13)
   B. Condemnation of Apostates (vv. 14-15)
      1. Warning from Enoch (v. 14)

Jude, the servant of Jesus Christ, and brother of James, to them that are sanctified by God, the Father, and preserved in Jesus Christ, and called: Mercy unto you, and peace, and love be multiplied (Jude 1-2).

13

SECURE IN CHRIST

**"...sanctified by God, the Father,
and preserved in Jesus Christ..." (v. 1).**

Lina Sandell Berg was no stranger to affliction. At the tender age of 12, she lay stricken with a paralysis that confined her to bed. Although physicians had all but given up, God restored her to complete health one Sunday after a time of prayer. Fourteen years later, Lina watched her father fall overboard and drown when the ship in which they were sailing lurched forward. At 35, Lina married C. O. Berg, a wealthy businessman. The joy of their happy marriage was short-lived when their firstborn son died at birth.

In spite of everything she suffered—affliction, heartbreak, and loss—Lina wrote nearly 650 hymns, many of them expressing how secure believers are in Christ's love. One hymn, "More Secure Is No One Ever," aptly expressed this security. Two of the five stanzas go like this:

> More secure is no one ever
> > Than the loved ones of the Savior—
> Not yon star on high abiding,
> > Nor the bird in home-nest hiding.

> Neither life nor death can ever
> > From the Lord His children sever,
> For His love and deep compassion
> > Comfort them in tribulation.[1]

Saved people are eternally secure in Christ. Nothing will ever separate them from Him—not affliction, heartbreak, loss of a loved one, or times when they draw away from God's love.

With this thought in mind, Jude greeted the recipients of his letter by reminding them of their security in Christ, which will keep them secure in an age of apostasy. But before doing so, Jude gave a word concerning himself.

Servant of Christ

Jude identified himself as a "servant of Jesus Christ, and brother of James" (v. 1). As mentioned in the introduction to this section, he was also the half brother of Jesus.

Often a prophet has no honor within his own family or city (Lk. 4:24). This was true of Jesus, for Jude rejected Him as Messiah early in His ministry. Sometime after Christ's resurrection, however, the scales fell from his eyes, and Jude came to faith in Christ (Acts 1:14).

Jude became so committed that he called himself a "servant of Jesus Christ" (v. 1). The word *servant* means *bond slave*. A bond slave had been released from slavery but, out of love for his master, voluntarily put himself in servitude to him for life. To show that he was a bond slave, the servant had his ear bored through with an awl against the door of his master's house (Dt. 15:17).

Jude's service reflected that of a bond slave. He chose to serve Christ out of love rather than force. His only desire was to do Christ's will, not his own. With undivided allegiance, he served Christ and no other master. His commitment was for life. This should be the attitude of all people who consider themselves to be servants of Christ. Often, however, the opposite is true. Many people in the ministry drop names, jockey for position in religious organizations, and befriend successful spiritual leaders to gain higher positions.

There are several possible explanations as to why Jude failed to identify himself as Jesus' half brother. First, Jesus was God, and Jude may have felt unworthy to be placed on the same level with Him. Second, Jesus considered everyone who did the will of God to be His brothers and sisters (Mt. 12:46-50). Third, it would not have been in keeping with Christian humility to make such a claim. Fourth, Jude initially rejected Jesus' Messiahship (Jn. 7:5) and did not receive Him until after His resurrection (Acts 1:14). Thus, he called himself a bond slave rather than a half brother of the Lord. Whatever the reason, Jude truly was a bond slave of Christ.

Selected in Christ

Jude was writing to those who had been "called" to salvation by God the Father (v. 1). Although the word *called* may appear to be misplaced at the end of the verse, rather than at the beginning, Jude put it there for emphasis.

The Bible mentions two kinds of calls concerning salvation. In the *general call*, God externally offers salvation to all mankind through Jesus Christ (Jn. 3:16). This call does not become effective until an individual receives Jesus Christ as Savior. Many people hear the gospel and are invited to accept the general call. Unfortunately, few do. Our Lord said, "many are called, but few are chosen" (Mt. 22:14).

The *efficacious call* takes place when God, through the Holy Spirit, irresistibly works on the mind and heart of a person He has chosen, so that the individual freely chooses to believe in Jesus Christ as Savior. Believers are called, not according to their own works, but according to God's purpose and grace (2 Tim. 1:9). Paul is a classic illustration of God's efficacious call. He was called, not according to his own will, but according to God's will (1 Cor. 1:1). In fact, he was bent on destroying the church until the moment of his call and conversion (Acts 9).

Sanctified for Christ

The moment a person heeds the call and becomes a Christian, he or she is "sanctified by God" (v. 1)—set apart, both spiritually (1 Cor. 1:1; 6:11) and physically (1 Th. 4:3), unto God for service. The sanctifying process takes place through the Holy Spirit, who cleanses believers by washing them with the water of God's Word (Eph. 5:26).

Scripture mentions three stages of sanctification. First, believers are *positionally* sanctified. They have been eternally set apart unto God by redemption through Jesus Christ (Heb. 10:10, 14; 13:12). Positionally, believers have been declared righteous before God through the imputed righteousness of Jesus Christ, which they received at the moment of belief. It is called *positional sanctification* because believers are considered holy in their standing before God.

Second, believers are *progressively* being sanctified. Progressive sanctification is an ongoing process in the daily walk of believers as they live out the teachings of God's Word. They must separate themselves from sin and allow the Holy Spirit to cleanse them daily by means of the Word of God. Jesus said, "Sanctify them through thy truth; thy word is truth" (Jn. 17:17).

Third, believers will be *perfected* in sanctification. They are promised an ultimate (complete) sanctification at the moment they receive their resurrected bodies. Paul said, "That he [Christ] might present it [the church] to himself a glorious church, not having spot, or wrinkle, or any such thing; but that it should be holy and without blemish" (Eph. 5:27). Then believers will be conformed to the image of Jesus Christ (Rom. 8:29), for they shall be like Him (1 Jn. 3:3).

Sanctification involves four agents. The Father chastens believers concerning their sin (Heb. 12:10). The Son provides the means for sanctification through His shed blood (Heb. 13:12). The Holy Spirit applies the truth of God's Word to believers' lives (1 Th. 2:13; 1 Pet. 1:2). Believers are to separate themselves voluntarily from sin. "Having, therefore, these promises, dearly beloved, let us cleanse ourselves from all filthiness of the flesh and spirit, perfecting holiness in the fear of God" (2 Cor. 7:1).

Although the Authorized Version (KJV) reads "sanctified," most Greek manuscripts use the word *beloved* instead. In the New Testament Greek language, the word *beloved* is a perfect participle, which means that God manifested His love to believers in a past act, and that love continues into the present. The believers to whom Jude was writing were loved by God the Father and were to be permanent objects of His love.

The Bible describes God's love in four ways. First, God loved believers in the past, before salvation: "But God commendeth his love toward us in that, while we were yet sinners, Christ died for us" (Rom. 5:8). Second, His love for believers is personal, like His love for His own Son. Jesus said, "thou...hast loved them, as thou hast loved me" (Jn. 17:23). Third, God's love is continually present with believers, as Jude taught: "who are loved by God the Father" (v. 1, NIV). Fourth, God's love is permanent for His own. Paul asked, "What shall separate us from the love of Christ?" He then answered by saying, "Shall tribulation, or distress, or persecution, or famine, or nakedness, or peril, or sword?...neither death, nor life, nor angels, nor principalities, nor powers, nor things present, nor things to come,

Nor height, nor depth, nor any other creation, shall be able to separate us from the love of God, which is in Christ Jesus, our Lord" (Rom. 8:35, 38-39). Now that's love!

Some scholars teach that believers can be separated from God's love and lose their salvation, but this is not scriptural. Believers are not only loved by God, but they have been "accepted in the Beloved" (Eph. 1:6), redeemed through Christ's shed blood (Eph. 1:7), and "sealed with that Holy Spirit of promise" (Eph. 1:13). It is impossible for believers to lose their salvation.

Secure in Christ

Today many Christians reject the idea that people can be eternally secure after they have received Christ. For such people, Jude stated unequivocally that believers are "preserved in Jesus Christ" (v. 1).

Grammatically, the word *preserved* is a perfect participle that means *to guard, to hold firmly, to watch,* and *to keep.* It speaks of a past act that took place the moment the person received salvation in Christ, with the present and permanent results of still being "preserved." Believers have been kept, are being kept, and will be kept as an eternal possession by Christ.

Many scholars teach that Christians can lose their salvation. This is not true. Believers are kept, not by their own power, but by God's power (1 Pet. 1:5), which provides the security necessary to preserve them in salvation. If Christians could lose their salvation, then salvation would depend upon them and not upon the keeping power of God. Christians are as secure in their salvation as the power of God is to keep them secure.

There are several Scriptures that prove beyond a doubt that redemption is a once-for-all divine act that cannot be reversed. First, Scripture teaches that people who have been regenerated by God "have everlasting life" (Jn. 3:16). This means that believers have eternal life as a present and permanent possession.

Second, Jesus stated that believers "shall never perish, neither shall any man pluck them out of my hand" (Jn. 10:28). The word *never* is a double negative in Greek and means *under no condition* will believers ever perish (lose their salvation).

Third, Jesus said that He keeps all whom the Father has given to Him, and He will lose "none of them...but the son of perdition" (Jn. 17:12). If it is possible for a person to possess salvation and then lose it, Jesus' words are untrue and cast suspicion on other statements He made about salvation.

Fourth, believers are "sealed with that Holy Spirit of promise" (Eph. 1:13). God the Father seals Christians into Christ by the Holy Spirit at the moment of conversion. That sealing is a once-for-all act that takes place at salvation and is irreversible. The sealing work of the Holy Spirit signifies several things. It authenticates the genuineness of a person's salvation (Eph. 1:13), denotes ownership and identifies the person as God's possession (Rev. 7:3), and guarantees that the person is eternally secure until the day of redemption (Eph. 4:30).

Sustained by Christ

All believers are blessed by God, especially those who must contend for the faith in an age of apostasy. For this reason Jude prayed that those to whom he was writing would have God's "Mercy...peace, and love...multiplied" (v. 2) to them.

Mercy is the manifestation of God's pity and compassion to people in distress and is kin to His grace. In God's divine order, His mercy comes before grace—He acts in grace because He has mercy for the plight of His people. It is God's mercy that will support believers who must face the persecution poured out against them when they stand for truth in an apostate age.

Mercy produces peace in the hearts of believers. People who have made peace *with* God receive peace *from* God, which produces the peace *of* God in their lives. This peace of God produces inner stability to face the pressures of an apostate age.

People who possess God's mercy and peace will also have His divine love. God's divine love, abundantly poured out, strengthens believers, enabling them to stand and earnestly contend for the faith during days of apostasy. How true the words of Lina Berg: "More secure is no one ever than the loved ones of the Savior"!

ENDNOTES

[1] Kenneth W. Osbeck, *101 More Hymn Stories* (Grand Rapids: Kregel, 1985), pp. 186-88.

Beloved, when I gave all diligence to write unto you of the common salvation, it was needful for me to write unto you, and exhort you that ye should earnestly contend for the faith which was once delivered unto the saints. For there are certain men crept in unawares, who were before of old ordained to this condemnation, ungodly men, turning the grace of our God into lasciviousness, and denying the only Lord God, and our Lord Jesus Christ (Jude 3-4).

14

CONTENDING FOR THE FAITH

"...contend for the faith which was once
delivered unto the saints" (v. 3).

The emergence in recent years of heretical religions is
phenomenal. An estimated three thousand man-
made, Eastern, philosophical religious systems have
sprung up throughout America. They are gaining followers by the thousands. The nation is being bombarded with
books on yoga, Hare Krishna, transcendental meditation,
reincarnation, spiritism, astrology, the New Age movement, and all of the other traditional cultic religions that
have always been present.

If you think that the teachings of these religions have
not had an impact on the church, think again! An author
recently wrote, "The New Age movement...involves things
that are firmly entrenched within the church, such as psychotherapy, visualization, meditation, biofeedback,

Positive Confession, Positive or Possibility Thinking, hyp-
nosis, holistic medicine, and a whole spectrum of self-
improvement and success-motivation techniques."[1]

Radio and television broadcasts propagating several of
these concepts fill the airwaves. Christians by the millions
send for literature from these groups and are being subtly
and unconsciously conditioned to believe in and practice
their antibiblical teachings.

Many seminaries are turning out graduates who are
more anti-Christian than Christian. "*Redbook* magazine
indicated that of the ministers in training represented in all
the major seminaries, 56 percent rejected the virgin birth of
Jesus Christ, 71 percent rejected that there was life after
death, 54 percent rejected the bodily resurrection of Jesus
Christ, and 98 percent rejected that Jesus Christ would
return to earth."[2]

The seeds of heresy are blowing throughout the land,
and many are finding fertile ground and germinating within the church. This is not new. The church faced the same
heretical teachings during its infancy. Heresy was so
prevalent in the first century that Jude was moved to pen
an epistle warning the church about false teachers and
encouraging it to earnestly contend for the faith.

Common Faith

Jude had planned to write about the "common [shared]
salvation" he and his "Beloved" brethren had experienced.
He had given "all diligence [haste]" (v. 3) to do so, but the
Holy Spirit intervened and compelled him to write about
heresy. Jude would much rather have penned an uplifting
epistle on the blessings of salvation, but he intuitively knew
the voice of God and responded according to His direction.

People filled with the Holy Spirit discern the direction
God desires them to take, even though it means changing
their plans. They want their plans to coincide with God's

will and are not afraid to tackle the difficult ministries God calls them to perform. Like Jude, they respond to God's voice and boldly warn those they love of impending trouble.

Contending for the Faith

Jude exhorted the church to "earnestly contend for the faith" (v. 3). The words *earnestly contend* are used to describe athletes locked in a vigorous, agonizing struggle for victory.

When the professional football play-offs are underway, each team wages an agonizing and determined struggle to beat its opponent. The same is true of Christians. They are in a spiritual war against satanic opposition (Eph. 6:13), but it is not a game. It's for life.

Like football players, who must wear protective equipment, Christians must strap on their spiritual armor for protection against the onslaughts of satanic attacks. Only then will they be able to stand their ground and win the battle.

All Christians must put on the spiritual armor described in Ephesians 6:13-17. First, they must have their "loins girded [wrapped] about with truth" (v. 14). The truth of God's Word supports and strengthens in battle and holds together all of a Christian's equipment. Without God's truth, Christians will be defeated by the enemy. Second, they need the "breastplate of righteousness" (v. 14), which protects the heart from embracing heresy, for out of the heart proceed "the issues of life" (Prov. 4:23). Third, they must have their "feet shod with the preparation of the gospel of peace" (v. 15). Believers prepared with the gospel will stand firm against the onslaughts of false doctrine. Fourth, "the shield of faith" (v. 16) quenches the fiery darts of the wicked. A never-ending bombardment of heresy from all directions confronts Christians daily, and only faith can shield them. Fifth, Christians are to "take the helmet of salvation" (v. 17). This helmet protects the mind, which is the seat of belief. Christians who understand and hold to the doctrine of salvation will have their minds protected from heretical teaching. Sixth, they must take up the offensive "sword of the Spirit, which is the word of God" (v. 17). Christians can obstruct and repel heresy only by using God's Word. They must read it, study it, memorize it, and meditate upon it if they expect to use it effectively. Christians can stand in battle only by putting on the *whole* armor. Football players would not consider playing without their helmets, shoes, or pads.

When Jude spoke about "the faith" in verse 3, he was not referring to an individual's personal faith in Christ but to the doctrinal truth that had been "once delivered unto the saints." The faith once for all deposited to the church during the apostolic period must be kept, managed, and guarded against change or error.

Several church groups, however, do not hold this position. The Roman Catholic church teaches that the basis for ultimate authority rests in the church and not in the Word of God. Final authority for the revelation from God is invested in the pope and the traditions of the Roman Catholic church. Thus, it claims that God still gives revelation today through the pope and the church.[3]

The Mormons hold a similar view concerning the Scriptures. "Former U.S. Senator Wallace Bennett, in his book, *Why I Am a Mormon*, said, 'We must recognize the Bible's limitations as well as its value. We do not ascribe final authority to any of its statements....Obviously, we do not accept the idea that with the adoption of the present contents of the Bible the whole canon of scripture was closed for all time.' The Mormons reject the Bible as the infallible Word of God."[4]

People who hold the above views have corrupted God's Word over the centuries and have allowed heretical errors to be incorporated into their teachings. In addition to these groups, apostates, modernists, liberals, and other cultists have found their way into churches and have twisted the Word of God both secretly and openly. In so doing, they have destroyed the truth of Scripture.

If Christians are to contend for the faith, they must study the doctrines of Scripture. Unfortunately, many Christians believe that doctrine is to be known only by ministers or seminary students, not by the people in the pews. These Christians are soft-minded and uninterested in the Scriptures and would be hard-pressed to tell others what they believe concerning the doctrines of God, Christ, the Holy Spirit, sin, grace, regeneration, justification, sanctification, or last things. Consequently, they are "tossed to and fro...with every wind of doctrine" (Eph. 4:14). They easily fall prey to the myriad of false teachings being proclaimed in churches today.

The logic is inescapable. If believers do not know doctrine, how can they stand for the faith? If they cannot stand for the faith, their personal faith will be overthrown. It is the duty of every generation to guard the faith. Failure to do so could mean that the next generation of Christians might not have a faith.

Corruption of the Faith

Jude wrote this epistle to warn Christians about false teachers who had crept into the church unawares (v. 4). Many scholars believe that these teachers were the Gnostics of the first century. The word *gnostic* means *knowledge*. The Gnostics claimed to possess secret knowledge that transcended the material world. They drew their beliefs from Greek, Egyptian, Persian, and Indian philosophies. Because they claimed to possess esoteric metaphysical insights, their beliefs could not be verified by observation. Their goal was to reduce Christianity to a mere philosophy and incorporate it into other pagan beliefs to which they subscribed.

The Gnostics believed that God neither created nor governed the universe and that He lived totally separate from it. The God of the Jews and Christians was an inferior being they called *Demiurge*. They believed in a supreme being who is the absolute, unknown, and ineffable one of whom nothing can be predicted. They also believed that the created world (all matter) was evil and totally separated from and in opposition to the spirit world. They further believed that Jesus was a mere man possessed by the heavenly Christ, who was the brightest of all *aeons* (*emanations from Bythos*). This heavenly Christ acted in the man Jesus but was never incarnate. The Christ returned to heaven before Jesus' crucifixion; thus, only a man died on the cross.

There also were divisions among the Gnostics. One group, the Libertine Gnostics, practiced moral excess. If, they reasoned, the flesh is evil but the "true person" is good, why not permit the flesh its excesses, for it cannot corrupt the true person who is the Spirit? Most likely it was the Libertine Gnostics to whom Jude referred in verse 4. Gnosticism was a wicked system of religious beliefs that flooded the church but died out within 150 years.[5]

Jude said that these heretics "crept in [the church] unawares" (v. 4). The word *crept* is used only here in the New Testament and means *to slide in alongside of*. They secretly came in like a person slipping through a side door and settling into a pew without being noticed. One writer put it well when he said that these false teachers seep gradually into the minds of the people by secret, stealthy, and subtle intrusion with the intention of undermining and breaking down their belief structure and conviction.[6]

Satan knew he could not destroy Christ's church (Mt. 16:18), so he tried to corrupt it through the infiltration of false teachers. His main method was to sow tares (false teachers) among the wheat (Mt. 13:24-30). Paul said that Satan's ministers were "transformed as the ministers of righteousness" (2 Cor. 11:15). They would change their outward appearance to look like something entirely different from their true nature. Such people are very dangerous because they seductively lead other people into false doctrines (1 Tim. 4:1).

Paul mentioned two groups that succumb to heretics more than others. The first group consists of churches that have "a form of godliness, but denying the power of it" (2 Tim. 3:5). These churches manifest the outward appearance of Christian commitment and moral goodness but are easy prey for false teachers because they disown the power of God. Second, "silly women laden with sins" (2 Tim. 3:6) are easy prey as well because their carnality, gullibility, and immaturity make them more open to the flattery and deceptive speech of heretics. Such people have itching ears to learn, but, being unable to discern truth from error, they embrace every heresy they hear. False teachers look for the homes and churches of weak-willed and spiritually unlearned people because they are more gullible and vulnerable to their control. For this reason, many cults go from house to house peddling their heresy.

Such people should not take the church by surprise. We should expect them to invade the church, for they "were before of old ordained to this condemnation" (v. 4). The word *ordained* leads people to believe that God chose these people to be false teachers, and therefore they had no choice in the matter. This is not the case. The word *ordained* means *to write beforehand*. God had revealed, almost from the beginning of mankind, that such teachers would come. Enoch, "the seventh from Adam" (v. 14), predicted that ungodly teachers would come and be judged by the Lord (v. 15).

Conduct of False Teachers

Jude described the nature of these false teachers in three ways. First, they were destitute of godliness, being called "ungodly" (v. 4). They were impious people lacking reverence for God. Their character and conduct manifested irreverence (vv. 8, 10, 16, 18).

Second, they debased grace, "turning the grace of our God into lasciviousness" (v. 4). The word *lasciviousness* has been translated in various ways: *wantonness, licentiousness, lawlessness, license, immorality,* and *sensuality.* These heretics committed unbridled sexual sins with no sense of shame. Nor were they fearful or concerned about others seeing them. These debased teachers put unbridled sexual sin in place of God's grace—a sin too gross to talk about.

Third, they denied the Godhead. Jude said they denied (disowned) "the only Lord God, and our Lord Jesus Christ" (v. 4). The word *God* is omitted in most Greek manuscripts, making the text read "our only Lord [Master], and our Lord Jesus Christ." Commentators are divided about whether God the Father and Jesus Christ the Son are both objects of denial, or just the Son. The first use of *Lord* (*despotes*) means *master* and denotes one with absolute or unlimited sovereign power. Most likely Jude meant that both the Father and the Son were being denounced by the Gnostics, as already discussed.

Gnostics were not the only ones who denied the teaching of a triune God. Today many groups—such as Jehovah's Witnesses, Unitarians, Jesus Only, Mormons, The Way International, Moon's Unification Church, and Christian Science—either corrupt or deny the triunity of God.

Dr. S. Maxwell Coder mentioned four truths about Christ that these false teachers deny. They deny Him as *Sovereign of the universe.* But He is the Lord (Master, v. 4) who spoke creation into being and holds it together with His almighty power. They deny His *Lordship.* But He is called *Lord* (*kurio,* v. 4), which speaks of His deity and sovereign rulership in the affairs of mankind and which demands mankind's obedience. They deny Him as *Savior.* But He is Jesus (v. 4), which means *Savior,* a name that shows the purpose of His incarnation (Mt. 1:21). They deny Him as the Christ. But He is the Christ (*Messiah, Anointed One*, v. 4), an official title that speaks of His messianic deliverance and world rule.[7]

Christian friends, we are at war! It is an agonizing, life-and-death struggle against heretics and apostates who continually distort, deny, and try to destroy the true faith. Such a struggle calls for total commitment by all Christians in the battle for truth.

Many years ago I received a stirring memo from The Friends of Israel home office. It expressed the kind of commitment required by Christians. The memo read:

> In October 1983, terrorists bombed the Marine barracks in Lebanon. Many Marines were killed and even more seriously wounded. The Commandant of the Marine Corps visited the hospital where the wounded were taken. His first stop was at the bedside of a young Marine who was at the very edge of life. An arm and a leg had been blown away; his body was a bloody mass connected to a life-support system. He could not speak; his vision was blurred. The Commandant bent low to whisper into the ear of this dying Marine. The Marine tried vainly to speak and then to write on the sheet with his remaining hand. A nurse quickly put a pen in his hand and held a tablet in place. The dying man wrote these words: "Semper Fi...." "Semper Fidelis" is the Marine Corps motto; it means, "Always faithful."

Christian friends, do you have the same kind of courage and commitment in contending for the faith as did that young Marine in standing for his country?

ENDNOTES

[1] David Hunt and T. A. McMahon, *The Seduction of Christianity* (Eugene: Harvest House Publishers, 1985), p. 8.

[2] T. Wilson Litzenberger, *Starting Trends in Our Generation*, "Religion" (Broadview: Gibbs Publishing, 1974), pp. 172-73.

[3] Harold J. Berry, *Exposing the Deceivers*, "Roman Catholicism" (Lincoln: Back to the Bible, 1985), p. 52.

[4] *Ibid.*, "Mormonism," p. 46.

[5] Alexander M. Renwick, *Baker's Dictionary of Theology*, "Gnosticism" (Grand Rapids: Baker Book House, 1960), pp. 237-38.

[6] Raleigh Campbell, *Expository Notes on the Book of Jude* (Little Rock: The Challenge Press, 1981), p. 18.

[7] S. Maxwell Coder, *Jude: The Acts of the Apostates* (Chicago: Moody Press, 1958), p. 24.

I will, therefore, put you in remembrance, though ye once knew this, that the Lord, having saved the people out of the land of Egypt, afterward destroyed them that believed not. And the angels who kept not their first estate, but left their own habitation, he hath reserved in everlasting chains under darkness unto the judgment of the great day. Even as Sodom and Gomorrah, and the cities about them in like manner, giving themselves over to fornication, and going after strange flesh, are set forth for an example, suffering the vengeance of eternal fire (Jude 5-7).

ANCIENT APOSTATES

**"I will, therefore, put you in remembrance,
though ye once knew this..." (v. 5).**

Apostasy is like a subtle viper that snares its victim
and slowly squeezes out its life. For this reason,
Jude reached back into the Old Testament and picked three
illustrations that would impact Christians concerning the
imminent danger they faced by falling away from the faith.

Jude prefaced his remarks by saying, "I will, therefore, put
you in remembrance, though ye once knew this" (v. 5). He
was going to remind them of biblical lessons so familiar that
they would not miss the point of what he was about to say.

The Failure of Israel

Jude recounted the failure of Israel as his first reminder
of apostasy. God had mightily delivered the Israelites from
Egypt. He had seen the affliction of Israel (Ex. 3:7), and,

after the Passover (Ex. 12:6, 29), 600,000 men with their families and the wealth of Egypt marched out of the land (Ex. 12:31-36). Israel had been saved from captivity by God, sheltered by the blood of the lamb, kept safe from judgment, and strengthened for their journey by feasting on the lamb, unleavened bread, and bitter herbs (Ex. 12:8).

God miraculously delivered Israel from Pharaoh's army as they passed through the Red Sea on dry ground. If the people had marched 50 abreast, the line would have stretched for 40 miles! Just as miraculous were the provisions for the 600,000 men and their families. By today's standards, it would take 30 boxcars of food and 300 tank cars of water to meet their daily needs.

Second, Jude mentioned Israel's unbelief. He said they "believed not" (v. 5). Israel failed to believe what God had promised them concerning Canaan. The leaders requested permission to spy out the land before entering it. Moses agreed and sent 12 spies to survey the land and its inhabitants for 40 days (Dt. 1:21-23). The spies returned paralyzed with fear and considered their conquest of the land impossible (Num. 13:32-33). Only Joshua and Caleb had faith that Israel would be able to defeat the enemy and possess the land as God had promised (Num. 13:30).

Third, Jude said that God "destroyed them that believed not" (v. 5). Because of Israel's unbelief, everyone 20 years of age and older died during the 40 years Israel wandered in the desert (Num. 14:29-34). It is impossible to determine exactly how many people died per day, but based on a 12-hour day, over a period of 38.5 years, there would have been approximately 85 funerals per day, or 7 per hour. What an awesome reminder of the price Israel paid for their disobedience to God.

Through unbelief, the people of Israel forfeited two things. First, they forfeited physical life, for God destroyed everyone who did not believe. The word *destroy* (Gr., *appollumi*) can mean either physical or spiritual death. Because it is used both ways, the context determines its usage. Here it refers to physical death and has nothing to do with Israel's salvation. Second, they forfeited the blessings of Canaan (Heb. 3:18-19). This is not a picture of forfeiting heaven (loss of salvation) but of destruction of the flesh.

The same is true for Christians, who are to judge sin in their lives (1 Cor. 11:29-30). Failure to do so could mean weakness, sickness, or even premature death, but never loss of salvation. There is also a sin that precipitates death for Christians (1 Jn. 5:16), but again there is no mention of loss of salvation. This is clearly seen in the case of Ananias and Sapphira, who died after lying to the Holy Spirit (Acts 5:1-11), but the passage does not say that they lost their salvation.

Some Christians find little or no value in studying the historic experiences of Israel recorded in the Old Testament because they have the final revelation of the New Testament. Paul taught the exact opposite: "Now all these things happened unto them for examples, and they are written for our admonition...Wherefore, let him that thinketh he standeth take heed lest he fall" (1 Cor. 10:11-12). Christians are to learn from Israel's history so that they will avoid the same pitfalls of unbelief. May it not be said that the one thing Christians learn from Israel's history is that they do not learn from Israel's history!

The Fall of Angels

Jude reminded his readers that even angels could fall. He recalled those angels "who kept not their first estate, but left their own habitation" (v. 6).

Three interpretations have been put forth to explain this passage. The first is that Jude referred to angels vacating the high position of habitation that God had designed for them—namely, heaven. They contend that that is all the text is saying, and nothing more should be read into it. But the passage teaches much more than that.

The second interpretation is that Jude referred to the angels (Rev. 12:7-9) who rebelled against God's authority when Lucifer tried to dethrone Him (Isa. 14:12-17; Ezek. 28:12-19). Again, the passage seems to describe much more than what occurred at Lucifer's fall. Furthermore, neither Satan nor the rebelling angels are presently "reserved in everlasting chains" (v. 6).

The third interpretation is that Jude referred to angels who left their habitation in heaven and, against their nature, committed sexual immorality with human women. This is the correct view for the following reasons. First, these angels were practicing the same sin as the men in Sodom and Gomorrah who gave themselves over "in like manner...to fornication" (v. 7). Second, they went "after strange flesh" (v. 7)—flesh of a *different nature*. Scripture clearly teaches this in the accounts of the men of Sodom and Gomorrah seeking sexual perversion with angels (Gen. 19:5) and other angels seeking the same with human women (Gen. 6:4).

Some scholars strongly object to this interpretation for the following reasons. Such a union would be abnormal, grotesque, and mythological. Jesus said angels are sexless and do not marry (Mt. 22:30). The phrase *sons of God* is also used to speak of godly men (Hos. 1:10; 11:1). The chapters preceding Genesis 6 contrast the godly descendants of Seth and the ungodly descendants of Cain (Gen. 4:16-5:32) and do not indicate angelic beings cohabiting with human women.[1]

The following facts support the interpretation that the sons of God are fallen angels. The Hebrew phrase *bene-elohim* (*sons of God*) in the Old Testament always refers to angels (Job 1:6; 2:1; 38:7; Dan. 3:25).

In Matthew 22:30 Jesus was talking about angels in heaven, not fallen angels on earth in Noah's day. It is true that angels are not able to cohabit and procreate among themselves, but they are able to take on human form and perform human functions, such as eating, walking, talking, and sitting. As already shown, angels were mistaken for men and were desired for homosexual acts (Gen. 19:5). Because the total nature of fallen angels is unknown, it may be possible that they cohabited with human women in Noah's day. This seems to be the case in Jude 6-7.

The Hebrew word *nephilim* (translated "giants" in Gen. 6:4) should be translated "fallen ones." It designates the unusual offspring of the unholy union of fallen angels and human women. Again, Jude taught that the angels committed sexual perversion by uniting with flesh of a different nature (Jude 6-7).[2]

Jewish history taught this position. The Jewish historian Josephus wrote, "Many angels accompanied with women, and begat sons that proved unjust" (*Antiquities 1:3:1*). The early church held this view until the fourth century, at which time the angelic interpretation was replaced with an alternate view.

These vile beings who left their first estate are "reserved in everlasting chains under darkness unto the judgment of the great day" (v. 6). Peter stated that "God...cast them down to hell, and delivered them into chains of darkness, to be reserved unto judgment" (2 Pet. 2:4). They are confined and closely guarded in a dense, dark place. It would appear that all fallen angels will be confined to the eternal lake of fire at the Great White Throne Judgment (Rev. 20:11-15; Isa. 24:21-23).

Satan's purpose in perpetrating such perversions on the human race was, first, to corrupt the messianic line, which would have kept Jesus from becoming totally human, thus nullifying His redemptive ministry. Second, he tried to create a hybrid of angelic humans who would be unredeemable, again nullifying Christ's redemptive ministry.

In the midst of such sin, it was possible to learn who did or did not compromise his or her faith in God, for Noah was "just...perfect [uncontaminated]...and...walked with God" (Gen. 6:9). For 120 years he was faithful to the task God had given him of preparing the ark and preaching righteousness (2 Pet. 2:5) to his degenerate age (Gen. 6:5). God's testimony of Noah is twofold. First, he "found grace in the eyes of the LORD" (Gen. 6:8). Second, "Noah did according unto all that the LORD commanded him" (Gen. 7:5). How refreshing to find a person in an age of total apostasy who was unmovable in contending for the faith. In every age, no matter how apostate it may be, God has people who will not compromise their faith.

Fornication of Sodom and Gomorrah

Jude drew his third illustration of apostasy from the fornication of Sodom and Gomorrah (v. 7). Does that seem strange? It shouldn't. Christ foretold that the last days would be like the days of Lot (Lk. 17:28-30). In the last days, conditions will become like those in Sodom and Gomorrah.

The sins of those cities were "in like manner" (v. 7) to those of the angels. They indulged in passions contrary to nature, "going after strange [a different kind of] flesh" (v. 7). The words *giving themselves over to fornication* come from a Greek word (*ekporneu*), which means *a total giving of one-self to the sin*. This is the sin of homosexuality, which is strongly condemned by God (Rom. 1:27).

People who practice such sins will suffer "the vengeance of eternal fire" (v. 7). The word *vengeance* has the idea of *executing a judicial decision with punishment*. The punishment to be meted out is "eternal fire" or suffering in the Lake of Fire forever (Rev. 20:15). The Word of God is very clear that people who habitually practice sexual immorality will not inherit eternal life (Gal. 5:19-21; Rev. 21:8).

The sins mentioned here are being widely practiced in the United States. The fire of sexual freedom is being fanned by the legal status given to pornography, which is estimated to be an $8 billion-per-year business. More than 2.5 million people view pornographic movies each week at more than 800 adult movie houses or through 400,000 video cassette sales. This does not include the pornographic movies on cable television.[3]

Molestation is on the increase as well. "One in four girls will be molested by her eighteenth birthday; and one in three twelve-year-old girls in the United States will be sexually assaulted in her lifetime."[4]

Sexual freedom in the United States has caused an epidemic of sexually transmitted diseases (STD) that is sweeping the country. "According to the Federal Centers for Disease Control, the nation is in the grip of an STD epidemic that infects an average of 33,000 people a day. That figures to 12 million cases a year, up from 4 million in 1980. At this rate, one in four Americans between ages 15 and 55 eventually will acquire an STD."[5]

More shocking is that these practices are being tolerated by the church. David Hesselgrave, in the book *What in the World Has Gotten Into the Church?*, documents the above statements.

Following a decision by the (US) Episcopal Church's House of Bishops that it is inappropriate to ordain a practicing homosexual, the parent Church of England published a report urging fundamental changes in attitude toward homosexuals and recommending that they not be barred from priesthood.

The much-publicized Universal Fellowship of Metropolitan Churches claims to believe in salvation by faith in Christ alone while wholeheartedly embracing the gay lifestyle.[6]

Consider the case of formerly married Christian singles in a large California church. Only 9 percent of the men and

27 percent of the women have remained celibate in their single state. Of 203 singles interviewed, more than one-fourth of them rationalized their sexual conduct by affirming that "Christ wants us to live abundant lives; to me that includes sex."[7]

Many Christians are succumbing to the mores of society and are accepting things that God has condemned. Lot is a perfect example of what can happen to a righteous person (2 Pet. 2:7-8) who succumbed to a wicked society. His downfall began when he beheld Sodom (Gen. 13:10) and walked by sight, not by faith. Next he chose to dwell in the plain of Jordan (Gen. 13:11), a type of the world. He pitched his tent toward Sodom (Gen. 13:12), and soon afterward he was not only living in the city but was a judge at the city gate (Gen. 19:1). This was a position that required him to uphold the principles, practices, and privileges of the perverted people around him.

Lot was so lacking in character that he offered his two virgin daughters to the men of Sodom to spare his two guests (Gen. 19:8). His testimony was of little value to either his family or in-laws, who turned a deaf ear to his warning of impending judgment (Gen. 19:14). Even Lot himself was reluctant to leave and had to be dragged out of the city as judgment was about to fall (Gen. 19:16).

Lot ended up crouched in a cave, stripped of his possessions, position, family, and friends, in a drunken stupor and a dishonored state. His daughters committed incest with him, resulting in the births of Moab and Ammon, who became bitter enemies of Israel (Gen. 19:30-38). Lot's life was a total waste and produced a negative testimony to those who knew of his belief in God.

In dark times of apostasy, God has His luminaries of faith—people who will trust Him and live above the corruption of a decadent world. The antediluvian age had its Noah, who walked with God and remained uncontaminated by the sin around him. The patriarchal period had its Abraham, who did not pitch his tent toward Sodom but "looked for a city...whose builder and maker is God" (Heb. 11:10). Israel had its Joshua and Caleb, who believed the promises of God while others had no faith.

Remember, we can live above the snares of apostasy if we "seek...first the kingdom of God, and his righteousness" (Mt. 6:33).

ENDNOTES

[1] C. Fred Dickason, *Angels: Elect and Evil* (Chicago: Moody Press, 1975), pp. 222-23.

[2] *Ibid.*, pp. 223-24.

[3] *The Presbyterian Layman.*

[4] *Ibid.*

[5] *Pulpit Helps*, December 1986, pp. 32-33.

[6] David Hesselgrave and Ronald P. Hesselgrave, *What in the World Has Gotten Into the Church?* (Chicago: Moody Press, 1981), p. 56.

[7] *Ibid.*, p. 60.

In like manner also these filthy dreamers defile the flesh, despise dominion, and speak evil of dignities. Yet Michael, the archangel, when contending with the devil he disputed about the body of Moses, dared not bring against him a railing accusation, but said, The Lord rebuke thee. But these speak evil of those things which they know not; but what they know naturally, as brute beasts, in those things they corrupt themselves. Woe unto them! For they have gone in the way of Cain, and ran greedily after the error of Balaam for reward, and perished in the gainsaying of Korah (Jude 8-11).

16

ACTS OF APOSTATES

"...they have gone in the way of Cain...
ran greedily after the error of Balaam...
perished in the gainsaying of Korah" (v. 11).

He was born near Lynn, Indiana, on May 13, 1931.
At the age of 21 he pastored his first church. He
preached fundamental Christianity early in his ministry,
but eventually his message radically changed to a corrupt
form of Pentecostalism laced with spiritualism and bogus
miraculous healings. He even claimed to have raised more
than 40 church members from the dead.[1]

In 1973 he founded an agricultural colony in Guyana, South
America, which later deteriorated when many members defect-
ed because of his autocratic control and harsh treatment.
Ironically, an interfaith group voted him one of the 100 most out-
standing clergymen in 1975.[2] Most likely he received this award
because of his community involvement in social programs.

On November 18, 1978, the colony in Guyana was destroyed when more than 900 of the faithful members committed suicide by ingesting poison. When government authorities investigated the tragedy, the 47-year-old leader was found shot to death.

That infamous religionist, Jim Jones—one of the worst apostates in modern history—is not an exception to the rule. J. Gordon Melton, in his book on American cults and sect leaders, has profiled numerous modern apostates similar to Jones.

Faced with the same horrible situation in his day, Jude profiled the characteristics Christians should look for in detecting present-day apostates.

Defiled Dreamers

Jude described apostates in three ways. First, they are dreamers who "defile the flesh" (v. 8). The noun *dreamers* refers to the sensual fancies that have contaminated these heretics, causing them to commit gross immoral acts similar to the sins of Sodom and Gomorrah. One author wrote:

> There is a pattern of sexual impropriety in the lives of many present-day cult and occult leaders. Sun Myung Moon was briefly imprisoned...in 1955 on charges of injuring public morals (i.e., sexual promiscuity)...David Berg's...flirty fishing, in which female members are encouraged to become "happy hookers"...if necessary, to demonstrate God's love to potential converts...Jim Jones regularly had sexual relationships with members of his congregation...involving both married and single individuals.[3]

Second, they "despise dominion" (v. 8). The word *dominion* (*kuriotes*) comes from the Greek for Lord (*kurios*) and is used of angels as well (Eph. 1:21; Col. 1:16). These apostates despised or rejected the authority of Christ and His angelic host. They became autocratic authorities and would not accept guidance from spiritual leaders (cp. Jude 4). *Dominion* can apply to *political authority* as well. Thus, these apostates rejected and rebelled against both church and state.

Modern apostates often conflict with the state, church, and families of their followers. They violate state laws in their practices of illegal political activities and fund-raising programs. Their doctrines twist and misinterpret biblical theology held by the local church. These leaders demand total loyalty and require their followers to break off former relationships with parents and spouses who might compete with their commitment to the movement.

Third, they degraded dignities by speaking evil of them. The words "speak evil" (v. 8) mean *to blaspheme*, whereas "dignities" refers to *glory*. Thus, these apostates slandered God and the angelic host in heaven. Many modern apostates blaspheme the Lord by their beliefs.

> Jim Jones claimed that he was the reincarnation of...Jesus Christ...Guru Maharaj Ji...had no reservations about accepting the rather exalted title of Perfect Master and Lord of the Universe...Sun Myung Moon has left little doubt in the minds of many of his disciples that he is the Messiah.[4]

Dr. Edward Pentecost put it well: "These three actions reveal their inner attitude of physical immorality, intellectual insubordination, and spiritual irreverence."[5]

Disputing the Devil

Jude contrasted the despised and degrading speech of these apostates with the self-restraint of "Michael, the archangel, when contending with the devil...about the body of Moses" (v. 9).

The archangel Michael's name means *Who is like unto God?* What a striking contrast to the name Satan, which means *adversary*, describing his opposition to God and everything that is holy. Michael is the warring angel (Dan. 10:13; Rev. 12:7) who protects Israel (Dan. 12:1) from Gentile world powers bent on its destruction. These references show that Satan will stop at nothing to destroy both God's people and His ultimate kingdom promises made to Israel.

We cannot be sure when the incident between Michael and Satan occurred because it is not mentioned elsewhere in the Bible. A number of church fathers wrote that Jude took the incident from *The Assumption of Moses*, a pseude-pigraphical writing in the Apocrypha that describes Moses' funeral, mentioned in Deuteronomy 34:5-6. Jude's state-ment is similar to that recorded in *The Assumption of Moses*, but there is no proof that this was his source. We do not know where Jude received his information. Some believers are puzzled as to why Jude introduced a noncanonical, tra-ditional story from the Apocrypha into God's revelation, if indeed he did. It must be understood that if Jude did quote from this Apocryphal source, he was not claiming it to be divinely inspired. The Apocrypha was never considered by Judaism to be divinely inspired, nor was it accepted as part of the Hebrew Bible. If Jude did quote from the Apocrypha, he was simply using a story familiar to his readers to illustrate the contention between Michael and Satan. Jesus, Stephen, and Paul also used noncanonical material not found in the Old Testament.

Why was Moses' body so important to Satan? Josephus wrote that Moses exceeded all men in understanding, mili-tary ability, and prophetic office. Josephus said that to those who heard him speak, it was as if they had heard the voice of God Himself.

It is not difficult to surmise that if Satan could have acquired Moses' body, he could have made Israel venerate and worship it. Not only would this be true of Israel; church history is replete with examples of people worship-ing images and religious relics. During the Tribulation,

Satan will persuade people to worship an image of a man (Rev. 13:4-5, 15).

Everything we know about Moses' burial is recorded in Deuteronomy 34:6: "And he [God] buried him in a valley in the land of Moab, over against Beth-peor; but no man knoweth of his sepulcher unto this day."

In responding to Satan, "Michael...dared not bring against him a railing [slanderous] accusation" (v. 9). He did not answer Satan with reproachful words that would pronounce judgment against him. He simply said, "The Lord rebuke thee" (v. 9), or, *May the Lord rebuke thee*—a wish for God to judge Satan.

We can learn several lessons from Michael's action. First, he did not usurp authority over God but left judgment to Him, as taught in Scripture. Christians are instructed to do likewise: "judge nothing before the time, until the Lord come, who both will bring to light the hidden things of darkness, and will make manifest the counsels of the hearts" (1 Cor. 4:5).

Second, when Jesus was tempted by Satan, rather than engage in dialogue with or rebuke him, He simply quoted the Word of God (Mt. 4:1-11). Christians are to resist Satan (Jas. 4:7) in like manner.

Third, during religious services, some ministers rebuke Satan and pronounce that, in the name of Jesus, his power has been broken and bound. The apostles were given a ministry of binding and loosing (Mt. 16:18-19) regarding the forgiveness of sin, but it was not used as mentioned here. If the archangel Michael dared not confront Satan, how presumptuous of Christians to do so.

Destruction Declared

In contrast to Michael, the apostates "speak evil of those things which they know not" (v. 10). They revile or blaspheme God, angels, and Christians (1 Pet. 3:16).

During the Tribulation, the Antichrist and his followers will do likewise (Rev. 13:5-6).

Jude went on to say that the apostates speak against those things that "they know not; but what they know naturally, as brute beasts, in those things they corrupt themselves" (v. 10). This verse contains two different Greek words for *know*. The first, *oida*, refers to mental comprehension of the spirit world. The second, *epistmai*, speaks of knowledge acquired by the senses—that is, by natural instinct (v. 10). The apostates are placed in the category of "brute beasts" (v. 10)—unreasoning animals that live by their senses because they possess no reasoning powers.

These apostates lacked true spiritual knowledge concerning the things of God. It was beyond their grasp because they were living by their natural senses and ungodly physical appetites, like the animal world. By their blasphemous language and unchaste lifestyle, they "corrupt [destroy] themselves" (v. 10). Thus, the apostates' Gnostic claim to possess esoteric spiritual knowledge was false.

Destiny Described

Jude chose three men from the Old Testament to illustrate how the apostates had rebelled against God's authority. The first example was the road of Cain: "For they have gone in the way [road] of Cain" (v. 11). In the account of Cain and Abel, each brother brought an offering to the Lord (Gen. 4:1-5). Abel's offering was a blood sacrifice, whereas Cain's was from the ground. God accepted Abel's offering because he gave it in faith, but He rejected Cain's offering, which was the work of his hands and given with an improper heart attitude (Heb. 11:4). When his offering was rejected, Cain became angry, his countenance fell, and he killed his brother Abel (Gen. 4:5, 8).

"The way of Cain" is a course in life that substitutes works for God's way of salvation. When God provided coverings of skins through animal sacrifices (Gen. 3:21), He taught Adam and Eve that blood was necessary for people to approach Him. Thus, "the way of Cain" is the practice of unregenerate mankind rebelling against God's way of salvation through blood, which in turn produces a religious system of self-willed worship by means of an individual's own works. This is clearly seen in many religious systems today.

The second illustration was the reward of Balaam: "For they...ran greedily after the error of Balaam for reward" (v. 11). The story of Balaam is found in Numbers 22-25; 31:8, 16. Balak hired Balaam (a hireling prophet) to curse Israel, but God prevented each of his attempts to do so. Realizing that he could not curse Israel, Balaam devised a plan whereby God would have to curse Israel. He had a Moabite woman commit harlotry with the men of Israel to seduce them into worshiping the gods of the Moabites (Num. 25:1-3). God did curse and judge 2,400 Israelites who worshiped Baal-peor (Num. 25:4-9), but, in the process, judgment fell on the Midianites (Num. 31:1-24) and Balaam (Num. 31:8), who had caused Israel to sin.

The "error of Balaam for reward" was his hiring out of religious services for monetary gain. The apostates in Jude's day did just that. They "ran greedily" after the money they could acquire by performing religious services (v. 11). "Ran greedily" means that they *poured themselves out* or *rushed impulsively* into this practice.

Today many religious leaders have accumulated great wealth by getting their followers to commit huge amounts of money to themselves and their movements. Sadly, many Christian television ministries, singers, and publishers seem to be performing religious services for wealth. Peter warned those who minister not to do it for "filthy lucre" (1 Pet. 5:2) or monetary greed.

The third example was the rebellion of Korah. Jude said that the apostates would perish "in the gainsaying of

Korah" (v. 11). The word *gainsaying* means *to speak against*. Korah—along with Dathan, Abiram, and 250 Levites—rebelled against and challenged the authority of Moses and Aaron as the only ones chosen to be mediators between God and the people (Num. 16). Actually, these men were rebelling and speaking out against God, who had put Moses and Aaron in positions of authority. That authority was validated when the earth swallowed up Korah, Dathan, and Abiram in judgment (Num. 16:31-33), and the 250 Levites were destroyed by fire (Num. 16:35).

In like manner, the apostates in Jude's day rebelled against three authorities: God's authority over their lives, Christ as their true Mediator, and the church leadership He had ordained. The word "perished" (v. 11) is in the past tense, showing that in God's eyes the apostates had already perished, indicating that their destruction was certain. Rebelling against God, Christ, or those He has set in positions of spiritual authority within the church is not to be taken lightly. God said, "rebellion is as the sin of witchcraft" (1 Sam. 15:23).

One author put it well when he said, "Cain rebelled against God's authority in salvation...Balaam rebelled against God's authority in separation...Korah rebelled against God's authority in service."[6]

Jude cried, "Woe unto them!" (v. 11). His words were not a curse or a wish for God's judgment to fall on the apostates, but an exclamation. His heart was stirred as he contemplated the precarious standing of these men before God and the horrible end that awaited them.

Many like Jim Jones have preached fundamental Christianity early in their ministries, only to deteriorate into apostasy. In a day of unprecedented temptation to compromise their testimony, whether it be in morality, money, or ministry, believers must be sober and vigilant to guard against a prowling Devil who seeks to destroy them.

Friend, is your armor in place? Are you contending for the faith?

ENDNOTES

[1] David G. Bromley and Anson D. Shupe, Jr., *Strange Gods: The Great American Cult Scare* (Boston: Beacon Press, 1981), p. 54.

[2] *Ibid.*

[3] *Ibid.*, p. 152.

[4] *Ibid.*, p. 129.

[5] Edward C. Pentecost, "Jude," *The Bible Knowledge Commentary* (Wheaton: Victor Books, 1983), p. 920.

[6] Warren W. Wiersbe, *Be Alert: Beware of the Religious Impostors!, 2 Peter; 2 and 3 John; Jude* (Wheaton: Victor Books, 1984), pp. 147-48).

These are spots in your love feasts, when they feast with you, feeding themselves without fear; clouds they are without water, carried about by winds; trees whose fruit withereth, without fruit, twice dead, plucked up by the roots; Raging waves of the sea, foaming out their own shame; wandering stars, to whom is reserved the blackness of darkness forever. And Enoch also, the seventh from Adam, prophesied of these, saying, Behold, the Lord cometh with ten thousands of his saints, To execute judgment upon all, and to convict all that are ungodly among them of all their ungodly deeds which they have ungodly committed, and of all their hard speeches which ungodly sinners have spoken against him. These are murmurers, complainers, walking after their own lusts; and their mouth speaketh great swelling words, having men's persons in admiration because of advantage (Jude 12-16).

17

UNMASKING THE APOSTATE

"...the Lord cometh with ten thousands of his saints,
To execute judgment upon...
all that are ungodly..." (vv. 14-15).

The winds of apostasy are raging worldwide. This is not new or startling, for the Bible predicted that in the last days apostates would flood the church with their heretical teachings.

Many Christians are confused about the distinction between an apostate and a heretic. The word *apostate* means *to fall away* or *leave* that which was previously believed or practiced in religion. Although the Hebrew and Greek words for apostasy are used only a few times in the Bible, its practice is seen in many passages.

In the Old Testament, Israel continually committed apostasy by leaving God and practicing idolatry. The nation was judged severely for its apostasy, but God continually offered Israel opportunities for reconciliation.

In the New Testament, apostates were people who professed to have accepted Christ but later denied His deity (1 Jn. 2:22), ceased to follow Him (Jn. 6:66-69), turned away from the faith because of persecution (Mt. 13:5-6, 20-21), or showed a lack of true belief in Christ by living in sinful rebellion against God (2 Pet. 2:20). These people may have *professed* to be Christians, but they did not *possess* salvation. In the last days, apostasy will become prevalent within the church (2 Th. 2:3; 1 Tim. 4:1; 2 Tim. 3:1, 5; 4:3-4).

The word *heresy* comes from a Greek word that means *to choose*. Heretics are true believers in Jesus Christ who choose to hold erroneous teachings that conflict with the orthodox biblical doctrines held by the church. There are two kinds of heretics within the church: those who are aware of their doctrinal error but still embrace and proclaim it, and those who hold heretical beliefs because they have not been shown the error of their ways.

In this section of his epistle, Jude made one final attempt to unmask the true character of the apostates and warn the church of their deceptive practices.

Character of Apostates

Jude began by presenting six word pictures to describe the apostates' character. He called their worthless worship "spots in your love feasts" (v. 12). The love feast was a Sunday evening meal brought to the local church, shared by all members, and concluded with the Lord's Supper. The meal was to be an expression of corporate love within the church, but it rapidly degenerated into drunkenness and disorder (1 Cor. 11:20-22) and eventually was held apart from the Lord's Supper.

The apostates had crept into these holy love feasts, spotting them with their defiled character and conduct.

The Greek word for *spot* can be translated *hidden rocks*, which was used from the time of Homer to denote a rock hidden just under the water's surface on which ships, unaware of the danger, crashed.[1] The church was to guard against such people, who would make spiritual shipwreck of their fellowship.

Second, Jude called the apostates wicked shepherds, for they were "feeding themselves without fear" within the church (v. 12). The word *feeding* means *to tend a flock of sheep, to shepherd*. The shepherd feeds, cares for, nurtures, and protects the flock. The apostate shepherds did the opposite by exploiting the sheep and gratifying their own appetites at the people's expense (Isa. 56:11; Ezek. 34:1-8; Jn. 10:12-13). They did it "without fear" (v. 12) or without realizing they were doing wrong.

Today there are many so-called shepherds (spiritual leaders) pretending to care for, nurture, direct, and protect Christians, when, in reality, they are fleecing the sheep. They build their own empires, living sumptuously from what the sheep provide and giving little or nothing in return. Amazingly, many Christians continually support such leaders, even when their immorality and financial irresponsibility have been proven. What a contrast to Jesus, the Good Shepherd, who cares for, nurtures, protects, and gave His "life for the sheep" (Jn. 10:11).

Third, Jude described the apostates as waterless clouds: "clouds they are without water, carried about by winds" (v. 12). Farmers in Israel were always in need of rain. They were encouraged when dark clouds appeared on the horizon promising rain to their thirsty fields. More often than not, however, their hopes were dashed when the winds carried the dark clouds past their fields without dropping rain.

So it was with the apostates, whose appearance, manner, and speech aroused great expectation. They seemed to be shepherds who could provide spiritual refreshment to thirsty souls, but the opposite was true. Because they lacked the water of God's Word, they left their hearers spiritually dry.

Many preachers say they can give spiritual refreshment, but their hearers remain thirsty. Their hollow messages on humanistic goodness, love, unity, principles for positive mental attitudes, methods to supposedly produce physical healing, and financial prosperity provide little refreshment for thirsty souls. Only the sound teaching of God's Word can quench people's spiritual thirst.

Fourth, Jude described the apostates as withered trees. The phrase "whose fruit withereth" (v. 12) is composed of two Greek words, *phthino* (*to waste away*) and *opora* (*autumn*).[2] Thus, it refers to autumn trees without fruit. Autumn is the time when fruit trees should be bowing over with fruit ready to be harvested, but these trees were fruitless. Because the time mentioned was late autumn, the trees were not only fruitless but leafless, giving the appearance of death.

The fruitless, leafless trees give a threefold picture of the apostates. First, they are "without fruit" or devoid of spiritual character and conduct. Second, they are "twice dead." Spiritually dead within, they give an outward appearance of their condition, as do leafless trees in late autumn. Jude was not teaching that these people were true believers who now were lost because of their apostasy. Rather, he was teaching that they were spiritually dead while they lived (1 Tim. 5:6). The Bible speaks of a "second death" in the Lake of Fire to be experienced by all apostates after the Great White Throne Judgment (Rev. 2:11; 20:6; 21:8). This will not be an annihilation of individuals, for they will be "tormented day and night forever and ever" in the Lake of Fire (Rev. 20:10). Third, they are "plucked up by the roots" (v. 12). In God's eyes, they had already been uprooted, judged, and their doom sealed. Rootless trees have no life and will never produce fruit. People without roots are like withered branches that are gathered and burned in the fire (Jn. 15:6).

A fruitful believer is pictured as a tree planted by a river, producing fruit at the proper season (Ps. 1:3). Only those connected to Christ, the life-giving vine, can produce spiritual fruit (Jn. 15:5).

Fifth, Jude described apostates as "raging waves" (v. 13) on a wind-tossed sea. Raging waves are wild, fierce, and untamable, depositing spewed-up mire and dirt wherever they flow (Isa. 57:20). This is a picture of the restless, untamed passions and appetites of apostates who constantly smash against barriers put in place by God to restrain and restrict their wickedness.[3] They spew forth shameful words and act like sea foam that has no substance. It rides on the crest of the waves until it hits a barrier and then vanishes.

Sixth, Jude described apostates as "wandering stars" (v. 13). He was not referring to the fixed stars by which travelers get their bearings. Rather, they were like bright meteors that streak across the sky and vanish quickly into the darkness of space, never to shine again. They give no light, direction, or guidance to travelers. Similarly, apostates appear on the scene with a big flash, professing to bring new light to spiritual pilgrims, but instead they guide people into deep darkness. Jude said that such people have their destiny sealed in hell. The word "reserved" (v. 13) denotes that their fate is firmly fixed forever. The intensity of their damnation is amplified by the words "blackness of darkness" (v. 13). People who follow such apostate teachers will suffer the same end.

Today many Christian leaders are thrust into the limelight and presented as luminaries of the truth to whom God has given special gifts to direct, teach, and heal the faithful. Christians flock to them, believing that God has given them special illumination or revelation that will bring extraordinary blessing to their lives. More often than not, however, such people prove to be fallen stars who streak across the religious world and vanish into disgraceful obscurity. We should be very careful about whom we believe, follow, and give our support. Apostates may seem to be bright lights at first, but they soon turn into fallen stars.

Condemnation of Apostates

Jude presented a word from Enoch concerning the Lord's judgment at His Second Coming: "And Enoch also, the seventh from Adam, prophesied of these" (v. 14). This is not the Enoch from the line of sinful Cain (Gen. 4:17), but Enoch the son of Jared, from Seth's line (Gen. 5:18-24). Enoch was a man of faith (Heb. 11:5) who "walked with God" (Gen. 5:22, 24) in close communion and fellowship for 300 years after the birth of his son Methuselah. His character and conduct testified against the corrupt and godless age in which he lived. He was a prophet who preached that the Lord would come and execute judgment against the ungodly of his day (Jude 14-15). He lived in total obedience to his Lord and "had this testimony, that he pleased God" (Heb. 11:5). Enoch's end was glorious: He "walked with God, and he was not; for God took him" (Gen. 5:24). The writer of Hebrews interpreted the meaning of "God took him": "Enoch was translated that he should not see death, and was not found, because God had translated him" (Heb. 11:5). The word *translated* means *to change* or *to be transferred to another place*. Enoch was bodily transferred from earth to paradise without experiencing death.

Enoch's translation to paradise is a picture of living Christians being raptured to heaven when Christ comes for His church (1 Th. 4:17). The two translations are not strictly the same because Christians will be in their glorified bodies after the Rapture, something Enoch could not experience prior to Christ's resurrection and glorification (1 Cor.

15:22-23, 51-53). The removal of Enoch before God's universal judgment on the antediluvian age is no doubt a picture of the church being raptured before the Great Tribulation.

Jude's statement concerning Enoch's prophecy is similar to one recorded in the Apocryphal book of Enoch (Enoch 1:9), which did not surface until the first century B.C. There are different views concerning Jude's quoting of Enoch. Many scholars believe that he quoted directly from Enoch. Some believe that Jude received the words directly from God. Others believe that he quoted an oral tradition about Enoch's writing that was circulating at the time.[4] Even if Jude had quoted from a noncanonical book such as Enoch, it does not prove that it is inspired or that Jude considered it inspired. Paul quoted from several noncanonical sources in his writings, but he did not endorse them. It is possible that the Holy Spirit led Jude to use a true statement concerning Enoch that was also recorded in the Apocryphal book of Enoch.

The first part of this prophecy dealt with the Second Coming of Christ: "Behold, the Lord cometh with ten thousands of his saints" (v. 14). There are several interesting truths revealed by this prophecy. The verb *cometh* (*came*) is in the past tense. Although the prophecy awaits future fulfillment, Jude stated it in the past tense to confirm and emphasize the absolute certainty of the Lord's coming. He is coming "with ten thousands of his saints" (lit., *an innumerable multitude* or *an unlimited number*). The *saints* (*holy ones*) will include angels, the church, Old Testament believers, and the Tribulation saints martyred for their faith. Notice that the prophecy began with "Behold," indicating that the reader is to pay specific attention to the eschatological coming of Christ.

One purpose for Christ's coming is to implement the wrath of God: "To execute judgment upon...all that are ungodly" (v. 15). Although this judgment will not be by a flood, as in the days of Noah, it will be universal in scope. The word *ungodly* is used four times to emphasize why these individuals must be judged.

Another purpose of His coming is "to convict all that are ungodly" (v. 15). He will present irrefutable evidence of their guilt, so that they are without appeal. The evidence will deal with two areas of their lives. First, "all their ungodly deeds" (v. 15)—those actions that came from their depraved nature—will be judged. Second, "of all their hard speeches which ungodly sinners have spoken against him" (v. 15) will be judged. The word *hard* means *harsh*, *stern*, *rough*, and *offensive* remarks made against Christ. God keeps records, and in the day of judgment people will have to give an account for every idle word they have spoken (Mt. 12:36). At the Great White Throne Judgment the books of people's deeds will be opened, and each person will be judged according to his or her works (Rev. 20:13).

Conduct of Apostates

In verse 16 Jude provided a summary of the apostates' ungodliness. First, they were "murmurers"—discontented people who grumbled in an undertone, muttering against God, believers, or anything that did not fall in line with his or her will.[5] Second, they were "complainers," or fault-finders—people who spoke out against the faults of others but did not recognize or acknowledge their own faults. Third, they were "walking after their own lusts," ordering their conduct after immoral desires that burned in their hearts. Fourth, they spoke "great swelling words," or bragged about themselves with great arrogance, using bombastic language to express their knowledge of God or spiritual things. Fifth, they held "men's persons in admiration because of advantage." They flattered influential people to impress them for personal gain, be it popularity, position, prestige, power, or profit.

Many Christians live like apostates. That is a strong statement, but it is true. They grumble under their breath against things that do not go their way. They find fault with others but are unwilling to recognize or admit their own shortcomings when pointed out by a Christian brother or sister. They live with immoral lust burning in their breasts and satisfy their desires in secret. Some brag proudly about their knowledge of God or spiritual things. Many flatter pastors or church leaders for personal gain.

As the church age draws to a close, apostasy will be manifested worldwide as never before. Jude has unmasked the character of apostates so that Christians can be discerning and avoid falling prey to the pitfalls of their distorted teachings and deceptive tactics.

We must make periodic checks on our commitment to guard against heretical teachings that could lead us astray. Jude would strongly warn: Be sure you possess salvation! Be sure you are grounded in sound biblical doctrine! Be sure your character and conduct measure up to a godly walk!

ENDNOTES

[1] Kenneth S. Wuest, *Wuest's Word Studies in the Greek New Testament:* Jude (Grand Rapids: Wm. B. Eerdmans Publishing Co., 1940), Vol. IV, p. 249.

[2] *Ibid.*, p. 250.

[3] D. Edmond Hiebert, "Selected Studies from Jude, Part II: An Exposition of Jude 12-16." *Bibliotheca Sacra* (July-September 1985), p. 243.

[4] Edward C. Pentecost, *The Bible Knowledge Commentary:* Jude (Wheaton: Victor Books, 1983), p. 922.

[5] Hiebert, *op. cit.*, p. 247.

But, beloved, remember ye the words which were spoken before by the apostles of our Lord Jesus Christ; How they told you there should be mockers in the last time, who should walk after their own ungodly lusts. These are they who separate themselves, sensual, having not the Spirit. But ye, beloved, building up yourselves on your most holy faith, praying in the Holy Spirit, Keep yourselves in the love of God, looking for the mercy of our Lord Jesus Christ unto eternal life. And of some have compassion, making a difference; And others save with fear, pulling them out of the fire, hating even the garment spotted by the flesh. Now unto him that is able to keep you from falling, and to present you faultless before the presence of his glory with exceeding joy, To the only wise God, our Savior, be glory and majesty, dominion and power, both now and ever. Amen (Jude 17-25).

VICTORY OVER APOSTASY

**"Keep yourselves in the love of God, looking for
the mercy of our Lord Jesus Christ
unto eternal life" (v. 21).**

In preparing for the Olympic games, athletes practice for hundreds of hours, toning their muscles and perfecting their skills. After years of rigorous physical training, mental hardening, and national competition, they are confident of victory. They enter the contest with their eyes fixed on one goal: Victory!

What is true of athletes can be said of Christians, but their test is not a game. They face the apostasy that the Bible predicted would flood the world in the last days. They also face psychics, mystics, and pseudo-religionists who propagate their bizarre teachings worldwide. Jude described their defiled character, deceptive teachings, and deplorable conduct to warn Christians to guard against them.

Rather than setting forth a defensive strategy to counter apostasy, Jude went on the offensive. He provided instruction that, if implemented by Christians, would assure them of victory over apostasy.

Reminding Believers

So often Christians are quick to forget the Word of God, leaving both themselves and the church vulnerable to heretical teachers. Satan enters with his apostate army, ready to snatch God's Word from the minds and hearts of believers. Therefore, Jude admonished the "beloved" (v. 17) within the church to remember three truths.

First, he urged them to recall "the words which were spoken before by the apostles" (v. 17) concerning apostates intruding into the church. Possibly the believers had heard firsthand the preaching and teaching of the apostles or had read their epistles. Whatever the case, they were aware of the apostles' warnings.

Second, he reminded his readers how prevalent apostasy would become "in the last time" (v. 18). The last time began with Christ's first advent and will conclude at His Second Coming. The apostles profiled the growing dangers of corrupt people and teachings filtering into the church in the interim.

Paul warned, "after my departing shall grievous wolves enter in among you, not sparing the flock. Also of your own selves shall men arise, speaking perverse things, to draw away disciples after them" (Acts 20:29-30).

Peter warned, "But there were false prophets also among the people, even as there shall be false teachers among you, who secretly shall bring in destructive heresies, even denying the Lord that bought them....And many shall follow their pernicious ways, by reason of whom the way of truth shall be evil spoken of" (2 Pet. 2:1-2).

John warned, "Beloved, believe not every spirit, but

test the spirits whether they are of God; because many false prophets are gone out into the world" (1 Jn. 4:1).

We must heed the apostles' warnings without delay. Failure to do so will leave the church without discernment and susceptible to a myriad of false teachings.

Third, Jude reminded his readers of the character and conduct of the apostates. They were scoffers, or mockers (v. 18), who scorned God's Word (2 Pet. 3:3), especially the promise of Christ's Second Coming (2 Pet. 3:4). They were sinful, walking "after their own ungodly lusts" (v. 18). They lusted to experience any new form of ungodliness that came their way. They caused schisms in the church by separating themselves (v. 19). Most likely they came in seeking to split the church or take it over. They were soulish, or "sensual, having not the Spirit" (v. 19). The word *sensual* refers to the soul. An unregenerate Adamic nature governed these people. Clearly, apostates are not Christians, regardless of how knowledgeable, articulate, and perceptive they may be, for they have "not the Spirit" of God. Paul put it simply: "Now if any man have not the Spirit of Christ, he is none of his" (Rom. 8:9). This admonishment is extremely important because many Christians who lack discernment are following teachers who are not involved in Spirit-directed ministries.

Responsibility of Believers

Christians can remain untainted by the many heresies manifested within and without the church today by taking Jude's command to heart: "Keep yourselves in the love of God" (v. 21). Believers are to keep (put a guard over) their lives in the sphere of God's love, so that they abide in the place of full blessing from the Lord. Jude did not say that God would stop loving Christians—that would be impossible (Rom. 8:35-39). It is possible, however, that failure to obey Christ (Jn. 15:9-10) may limit God from bestowing the fullness of His love and blessing.

Believers keep themselves in God's love by maintaining three practices. First, by "building up yourselves on your most holy faith" (v. 20). The words *building up* refer to building a superstructure on a solid foundation—that which was established at the time of salvation. This is done by adding to "faith virtue...knowledge...self-control... patience...godliness...brotherly kindness...love" (2 Pet. 1:5-7). The pronoun *yourselves* tells Christians that they are responsible for their own spiritual growth and must not rely solely upon their pastors, Sunday school teachers, or Christian leaders to provide it.   Growth comes only through in-depth study of and meditation on God's Word.

Second, Christians are kept in God's love through "praying in the Holy Spirit" (v. 20)—praying with dependence on the Holy Spirit (Rom. 8:26-27). The prerequisite of such praying is a Spirit-filled (controlled) life.

Third, Christians are kept in God's love when they anticipate the coming of the Lord: "looking for the mercy of our Lord Jesus Christ unto eternal life" (v. 21). The word *looking* means *to wait anxiously* for the coming of Christ.   Those who live with such hope are to manifest purity of life (1 Jn. 3:3).

The words *building up, praying,* and *looking* are in the present tense. Christians must continually follow these practices if they expect to be victorious over heretical teaching.

What a contrast between Christians and apostates. Christians who have received God's mercy await the Second Coming of Christ and will receive blessing at that time.   Apostates who have rejected God's mercy and scoffed at the Second Coming will receive judgment and damnation at Christ's coming.

Rescuing the Beguiled

Because God does not give up on those who embrace apostasy, Jude felt duty bound to instruct his readers to evangelize such people. To grasp what Jude is teaching, we need a more lucid translation of verses 22 and 23: "And have mercy on some, who are doubting; save others, snatching them out of the fire; and on some have mercy with fear, hating even the garment polluted by the flesh" (NASV).

Three types of apostates must be reached. First were the sincere doubters: show "mercy on some, who are doubting" (v. 22). Most likely these people had heard the claims of Christ and were close to making a decision, but they wavered because of intellectual confusion about what to believe. They had to be given the true gospel in love—something totally lacking in the apostates and their teachings.

Second were the denouncers—people who have heard the gospel but denounced it and embraced the apostates' teachings. Because they are in imminent danger of going to hell, Jude admonished "save others, snatching them out of the fire" (v. 23). Only God can save them, but He works through Christians to do so. There is a sense of urgency to pull or snatch them from the fire. The idea is to exercise strenuous and aggressive action in rescuing people from great danger, like snatching a person from a burning building.

What better illustration can be given than that of Lot and his family, who were snatched from Sodom by angels just before the city was destroyed in a rain of fire and brimstone (Gen. 19:15-16, 24). Israel is pictured as "a firebrand plucked out of the burning" (Amos 4:11; Zech. 3:2), or retrieved from the fire of destruction for God's purpose.

Third were those who are totally defiled: "and on some have mercy with fear, hating even the garment polluted by the flesh" (v. 23). These people are so polluted that there is little hope of salvaging them from apostasy. Nevertheless, Christians must attempt to save such people from damnation. When witnessing, Christians must love sinners but hate their sins. Sin is characterized by "garments polluted [spotted] by the flesh" (v. 23). *The flesh* speaks of a sinner's unregenerate sin nature. This can best be illustrated by a leper whose inner garment (tunic) worn next to the flesh has become contaminated by the disease. In like manner, apostates can contaminate everyone who comes in contact with them if proper precautions are not take. Therefore, Christians must deal with apostates "with fear" (v. 23) or caution—lest they become defiled by their teachings.

In these two verses Jude presented seven truths about evangelism.

1. People are lost and in need of salvation.
2. Salvation is provided only through Christ.
3. God uses Christians to reach the lost.
4. Christians must be on guard so that they do not become influenced by the false teachings of those they are trying to reach for Christ.
5. Christians must be aware of the heretical beliefs of apostates.
6. Unbelievers will be eternally consigned to flaming fire (Mt. 10:28; Rev. 21:8) if they reject Christ.
7. While apostates live, it is possible for them to receive Christ.

Reassuring Benediction

Jude concluded his epistle by focusing on God's glorious power to preserve Christians from apostasy (cp. v. 1). First, He has the ability to keep believers: "Now unto him that is able to keep you" (v. 24). The Lord is sovereignly in control of all things, and in His omnipotence He is able to deliver believers through their pilgrimage on earth. He is also "the only wise God" (v. 25); thus, believers can draw upon His omniscience (Jas. 1:5) to stand against an apostate age. Some translations of verse 25 read, "the only God, our

Savior through Jesus Christ" (v. 25). Jesus is the only Savior in the universe who is able to provide salvation and deliverance from wickedness. He is omnipresent—"both now and ever" (v. 25)—protecting believers from whatever harm Satan may bring their way.

Second, God has assured believers that He will "keep [them] from falling" (stumbling) [v. 24]. The word used here for *keep* is not the same word used in verse 21. In this instance it means *to preserve*. The word *falling* means *to stumble* while traveling along the pathway of faith. When believers wander down a wrong path or stumble over obstacles in their path, God will preserve them from destruction. He will see them through this evil world and present them "faultless before the presence of his glory" (v. 24). One day Christians will stand in God's presence clothed in Christ's righteousness, "not having spot, or wrinkle...and without blemish" (Eph. 5:27). On that day they will be filled with "exceeding joy" (v. 24). This assurance should produce exceeding joy in the heart of every Christian today.

Third, Jude ascribed adoration to God for what He has provided in Christ: "glory and majesty, dominion and power, both now and ever" (v. 25). *Glory* is the radiant shining forth of all that God is in Himself. The *majesty* of God is His regal greatness, splendor, and dignity as sovereign Lord. His *dominion* speaks of His unprecedented strength and power as sovereign ruler of the universe. *Power* refers to God's ability and authority to govern the universe. Knowing that there is such a God in the universe—one who has provided victory over apostasy to everyone who trusts in Him—what more can be said but "Amen" (v. 25)!

The Radio Bible Class in their booklet *What About Those Dangerous Religious Groups?*[1] has provided Christians with some very good ways to discern false religious leaders.

Ask yourself the following questions:

1. Are they characterized by reverence and humility or by brashness and arrogance (2 Cor. 10:1-18)?

2. Are they gentle, or are they demanding (2 Tim. 2:24-26)?

3. Do they show respect for other authority and power, including the Lord, parents, government, and even Satan himself (2 Pet. 2:10-12; Jude 8-10)?

4. Do they show respect and love for gifted Christian leaders (1 Cor. 3:1-19)?

5. Do they promote individual discernment, growth, and maturity in their followers, or do they foster dependence and submission (Acts 17:11; Eph. 4:11-16)?

6. Do they exploit their members financially, or do they do everything possible not to burden them (1 Pet. 5:2; 2 Pet. 2:3)?

7. Is there evidence of sexual faithfulness, or are they sensually indulgent (2 Pet. 2:14)?

8. Do they encourage separation from sin to God, or do they tighten the grip of evil on their members by telling them only what they want to hear (2 Tim. 4:3-4)?

9. Do they sacrifice their own interests for the well-being of their group, or are they carried like kings on their followers' shoulders (Phil. 2:3-4)?

10. Do they in practice draw the attention and allegiance of their followers to Christ, or are those just words they use while actually focusing attention on themselves (Acts 20:28-31; 3 Jn. 9-10)?

11. Do they abuse their authority, throwing their

weight around, or do they lead by information, encouragement, and example (1 Pet. 5:1-4)?

12. Do they adopt an authoritarian manner, or are they willing to be treated as brothers (Mt. 23:8-12)?

13. Are their groups loved and hated because of their personal faith and allegiance to Christ or because of the teachings and interpretations peculiar to the founder (1 Tim. 1:3-7)?

14. Do they keep their members by love, example, and teaching or by making them afraid to leave the group (Gal. 2:11-21)?

15. Do they meet the qualifications of a spiritual overseer, or are they gifted men of questionable character (1 Tim. 3:1-7)?

By asking these questions, Christians can discern if a particular religious leader or group is apostate or headed in that direction.

Are you in spiritual condition and confident of victory as you stand against apostasy? Only you know the answer to that question. Jude has set forth seven commands that, when followed, assure Christians of victory.

1. Earnestly contend for the faith (v. 3).
2. Remember the words of the apostles (v. 17).
3. Build yourself up in the faith (v. 20).
4. Pray in the Holy Spirit (v. 20).
5. Keep yourself in the center of God's love (v. 21).
6. Look for the coming of the Lord (v. 21).
7. Show mercy to the unsaved and share with them the gospel of grace (vv. 22-23).

There you have it! Paul and Jude have equipped you with the needed scriptural principles and illustrations to

properly guard the gospel of grace. Do you have a friend
or family member who is dabbling in a heretical teaching or
cult practice? What better time to show that loved one the
way to salvation, which can only be acquired through the
grace and truth of Jesus Christ.

ENDNOTES

[1] Martin R. DeHaan, II, *What About Those Dangerous Religious Groups?*
(Grand Rapids: Radio Bible Class, 1986), pp. 9-10.

RECOMMENDED READING

Coder, S. Maxwell, *Jude: The Acts of the Apostates* (Chicago: Moody Press, 1958).

Hesselgrave, David J., and Hesselgrave, Ronald P., *What in the World Has Gotten into the Church?* (Chicago: Moody Press, 1981).

Hiebert, D. Edmond, *Second Peter and Jude: An Expositional Commentary* (Greenville: Unusual Publications, 1989).

Ironside, H. A., *Exposition of the Epistle of Jude* (Neptune, NJ: Loizeaux Brothers, 1940).

MacArthur, John, Jr., *Beware the Pretenders* (Wheaton: Scripture Press Publications, Victor Books, 1980).

MacDonald, William, *Believer's Bible Commentary*, Jude (Nashville: Nelson Publishers, 1990).

McGee, J. Vernon, *Thru The Bible with J. Vernon McGee*, Jude (Pasadena: Thru The Bible Radio, 1983).

Pentecost, Edward C., *The Bible Knowledge Commentary*, Jude (Wheaton: Scripture Press Publications, Victor Books, 1983).

Wiersbe, Warren W., *The Bible Exposition Commentary*, Jude (Wheaton: Scripture Press Publications, Victor Books, Vol. 2, 1989).

Wuest, Kenneth S., *Wuest's Word Studies*, Jude (Grand Rapids: Wm. B. Eerdmans Publishing Co., Vol. 4, 1944).

ABOUT THE AUTHOR

DAVID LEVY was born and reared in Dayton, Ohio. He received Jesus as his Messiah through the witness of a Hebrew Christian in November 1960. He is a graduate of Moody Bible Institute, the University of Illinois, and Trinity Evangelical Divinity School. David spent ten years pastoring in Illinois.

Since 1974 David, along with his faithful wife Beverly, have been on the staff of the highly respected, New Jersey-based Friends of Israel Gospel Ministry. He serves as the Foreign Field Director, overseeing workers in nine countries. In addition to his administrative and personnel responsibilities, he is in demand throughout the world as a conference speaker. David travels extensively representing The Friends of Israel in Eastern and Western Europe, Israel, New Zealand, Australia, and North and South America.

David has been Associate Editor of The Friends of Israel's highly acclaimed bimonthly publication, *Israel My Glory*, since 1977. His expositional articles appear in each issue of the publication and in many other international magazines. He has authored a number of books including *Joel: The Day of the Lord*; *Malachi: Messenger of Rebuke and Renewal*; and *The Tabernacle: Shadows of the Messiah*.